PREND MOI TEL QUE JE SUIS

DUMBARTON OAKS

DUMBARTON OAKS

DVMBARTO

SOMNIA·SVB·PATVLIS·VID
SIDERA·FAVSTA·FERANT

TESTIMONI
BEATRICIS
NEC·ILLORVM·IMMEMO
VITAS·VERITATI·ERV
HANC·TABELL
ROBERTVS WOODS BL

MCMX

GARDEN INTO ART

Susan Tamulevich
Photographs by Ping Amranand
Foreword by Philip Johnson
Design by Massimo Vignelli

ON·OAKS

EANT·NASCENTIA·RAMIS
OMINA·ET·VSQVE·BONA
⎯⎯⎯⎯⎯⎯⎯⎯
·AMICITIAE
FARRAND
ES·QVI·POSTERO·AEVO
NDAE·IMPENDERINT
M·POSVERVNT
SS·VXORQVE·MILDRED

XXII

THE MONACELLI PRESS

*This book would not have been possible without the support of
Dumbarton Oaks.*

*First published in the United States of America in 2001 by
The Monacelli Press, Inc.
10 East 92nd Street, New York, New York 10128.*

*Library of Congress Cataloging-in-Publication Data
Tamulevich, Susan.
Dumbarton Oaks : garden into art / Susan Tamulevich ; photographs by
Ping Amranand ; foreword by Philip Johnson ; design by Massimo Vignelli.
p. cm.
Includes bibliographical references (p.).
ISBN 1-58093-069-7 — ISBN 1-58093-109-X (pbk.)
1. Dumbarton Oaks Gardens (Washington, D.C.). I. Amranand, Ping. II. Title.
SB466.U65D868   2001
712'.6'09753—dc21   2001044068*

Printed and bound in Italy

Graphic production: Piera Brunetta

*Endpapers: Ernest Clegg, watercolor map of Dumbarton Oaks, 1933.
Page 1: French eighteenth-century lead-on-wood plaque representing autumn
in the Orangery.
Pages 2–3: Cherry trees beyond the peony beds in the Cutting Garden in spring.
Pages 4–5: The North Vista in summer.
Pages 6–7: View from the Urn Terrace to the Rose Garden in autumn.
Pages 8–9: View from the Rose Garden toward the Orangery in winter, with
"Finalities" plaque to the right.
Pages 10–11: Tribute panel to Beatrix Farrand in the wall of the Green Garden,
installed in 1935.
Pages 16–17: Detail of the wheat sheaf atop the R Street gates,
which were designed by Ruth Havey and installed in 1954.*

Contents

To my parents, Barbara and Walter Tamulevich,
with love and gratitude
—S.T.

To my mother, who instilled in me
a love of gardens
—P.A.

Acknowledgments

This book is like the tip of an iceberg: what is here *unseen*—the support, the assistance with research, the friends who helped in countless thoughtful ways—is tremendous.

I would first like to thank Dumbarton Oaks's director Edward Keenan and director emerita Angeliki Laiou for granting Ping Amranand and me permission to pursue our work on the garden. The support of the staff at Dumbarton Oaks—in particular, archivist Dr. James Carder, librarian Annie Day Thacher, director of garden studies Professor Michel Conan, librarian in the rare book library Linda Lott, and superintendent of the garden Gail Griffin—has made this a pleasant, teamlike undertaking. The shared delight we all felt as new information came to the fore was occasionally almost intoxicating.

Peter Blake has been an invaluable adviser and critic of my work throughout the project. Philip Johnson encouraged me in my investigation of Mildred Bliss and permitted me to interview him on several occasions. When I struggled at the midway point, Donald W. Faulkner generously gave me insights as to reorganization, as well as a mysterious kind of sanction to continue.

My good friends in Washington, D.C., and Maryland have been hospitable on many visits. I would especially like to thank Raya Bodnarchuk, Tina and Michael Coplan, and Janice Frey.

In Maine, Eileen Ahern and Whitney Landon welcomed me several times as I explored Beatrix Farrand's past on Mount Desert. John Githens and Ingeborg Ten Haeft surprised me with the generous gift of a computer at a critical moment.

Finally, I would like to thank my parents for their confidence in me throughout this long process. They have made all the difference.

—S.T.

Foreword:
The Pavilion in the Garden
Philip Johnson

In 1958 Philip Johnson was asked to design a museum pavilion for the Dumbarton Oaks Library and Study Center. Lincoln Kirstein had recommended Johnson to the center's then director, Jack Thacher. Although hired by Harvard University, which administers the center, Johnson worked very closely during the design process with Dumbarton Oaks's founder and benefactor, Mildred Bliss. More than forty years later, he reflects on that experience.

The Dumbarton Oaks pavilion is the result of my collaboration with my patron, Mildred Bliss. She simply decided that I was to be a part of her life, in the same way in which (I am sure) she probably took over the designers of her garden, Rateau and Farrand. Mrs. Bliss and I were in love. I told her: this has got to be "Bliss and Johnson" as the architects, and we all laughed. I spent much more time on that job than I've ever spent on a comparable building since. That is why it came out so well.

I can't recall if it was my idea, or hers, to do a totally modern building. We just started working. It was her idea to build a full-scale mock-up of one of those domes. Can you imagine, building a whole one of those mock-ups—but complete? The model was done in wood while the real one would be of glass and stone and bronze. She had the mock-up constructed inside the concert hall at Dumbarton Oaks so that we could judge the shadows and every little detail. That's the degree she must have gone to when she discussed the design of the garden on the property.

She never engaged in the sort of criticism that clients usually do. She never said, "I want a little more of this and I'll have a little more of that." She said, "I want to come to you. You are the architect. Just call me when you need anything. I'm here; there's no budget." That's what an architect always remembers.

The thing was that she was not impressed by what I knew about her, but in what she knew about me, which was delightful and made our working together much easier. Yet it was curious that she should have liked pineapple finials and still cared for what we were doing together.

I was young then, and so I thought that her generous way of working was what architecture was all about; and it is not. Actually architecture can be a very unpleasant, struggling thing, but working with Mildred Bliss was sheer unadulterated pleasure. And it was much the same as working for myself.

The whole idea was to fit a small pavilion into a treescape that was already there. The building was to become a part of the Bosque, with the trees growing right up next to it; that's really all there was to it. The trees were absolutely sacred, to her as well as to me, and I used every tree. One of them I honored in particular, more than I should have—the tree where the passageway was to go between the new and old buildings. The construction around that tree was very carefully done—Mrs. Bliss was good at landscaping, and she knew exactly when I was encroaching upon the tree roots.

The museum that we built is not an "outside" building. It is to be seen from the inside. Why does the space seem bigger on the inside than it does from the outside? It is because of the glass walls, because you judge the space you are in by the nearest vertical element that you recognize, and in this case that is, of course, the trees in the Bosque. The trees give you the measure.

I didn't really know what was going to be exhibited in the museum. As a museum curator, which I was at the time, I should have realized that the building should have been a background to the objects. But the way I built it, all you see is the outdoors when you are inside the museum.

Above:
Interior of Philip Johnson's museum
pavilion for Robert Bliss's collection of
pre-Columbian art.

When Mildred Bliss was concentrating there was nothing else in the whole world except the design of this building. Take the choice of the marble. Our discussions on that were endless, but she said yes to my choices. And she said yes to the use of bronze for the trim. I never thought of function, and function was the ruling passion among architects at that time. My mind became so conditioned to her kind of approach that it never occurred to me to make any other kind of building.

She was most interested in the decoration. One important element to me and to her was the fountain at the middle of the building. It is made of slate turned on end, an idea I'd gotten from Lutyens. She liked materials: the bronze, the marble, the up-ended slate.

Before Dumbarton Oaks, I had been a pure Miesian. That building may have been my first postmodern building! It was the combination of daring design with the use of conventional, beautiful materials that made it all palatable to her. I guess she didn't even think of the building as modern, just as materials and shapes.

I like to say that the only good job I've done is the next one; but I think what I may be best known for is this little pavilion.

Introduction

At the top of the hill at the end of Washington, D.C.'s 32nd Street, N.W., in the midst of residential Georgetown, sits the estate known as Dumbarton Oaks. The original Federal-style house and surrounding ten acres of formal gardens, now owned by Harvard University, are situated in an area once referred to by city planner Carl Feiss as "America's most civilized square mile." The elegant tract scarcely betrays its recent history. For when Mildred and Robert Bliss bought the property in 1920, the land was still pastoral. It had been farmed for more than one hundred years: there were cow paths, barns, and even a wandering peacock.

To imagine what the place must have looked like even further back in time, it is necessary to wander down the street and into Rock Creek Cemetery, founded in 1719 and the oldest graveyard in the city. Tombstones jut like barnacles from the staggered slopes as they fall in short, awkward shelves toward Rock Creek to the northeast. This preserved landscape is one of the few remaining places where it is possible to sense what the land surrounding Dumbarton Oaks was like when it was only slightly tamed, at the start of the nineteenth century.

This book recounts the transformation of that ramshackle farm into the singular garden that is Dumbarton Oaks. It is largely the story of two women: Mildred Bliss, a sophisticated heiress, and the landscape gardener who became her friend and collaborated on the realization of her vision—Beatrix Farrand.

Like any living thing, a garden is constantly growing and changing, and Dumbarton Oaks had a long evolution before it reached its present mature form. Mildred Bliss began by designing the place herself, copying the fashion of her friends overseas, such as Edith Wharton and Bernard Berenson. In the early years of the twentieth century, both had purchased villas and chateaus and restyled them to fit their Edwardian fantasies. To these sophisticated individuals, the development of decor and gardens was an amusing and satisfying game.

For Mildred Bliss, that game was to become an endeavor. She had grown in Sharon, Connecticut, an idealistic New Englander, and always retained her love of woodlands and arcadian scenes. But as an adult and the wife of a diplomat, she traveled widely and often lived abroad, and her affections expanded to include the refinements of Old World estates. Her vision for the property was complex.

Beatrix Farrand was able to interpret Mildred Bliss's vision with real genius during the first decade of their association and then, like a faithful spouse, stood by and gritted her teeth as she bore Bliss's flirtations with other designers. Bliss continued on her own way in the late 1950s when, these forays went beyond Farrand's capacity for accommodation, and, with a great burst of energy and an even greater sense of independence, in the early 1960s, following Farrand's death.

The architect Philip Johnson was asked in 1958 to design a small museum pavilion in the garden at Dumbarton Oaks. He was among the last designers to work directly with the somewhat daunting Mildred Bliss, who, by his account, was both the impetus and final arbiter for all work done on the property. "It was all her doing," he said. "She was a *great lady*, and there were very few of those in America." Looking back on a career that has spanned more than half a century, Johnson considered Bliss the best client he ever had. He appreciated her perpetual willingness to rework ideas with him until the best design solution had been achieved, and also the fact that she never hesitated to use the finest materials. Working with the clear direction and full support and trust of a client can enable a designer to produce the finest work of which he or she is capable. Such was the case with both Philip Johnson and Beatrix Farrand at Dumbarton Oaks.

What mattered most in the garden's creation were the same design criteria most significant to other great works of art: a certain "rightness" and ease of expression—a characteristic of Beatrix Farrand's work—plus the "hand" or perceptible signature of its creator. Here, of course, it is of that "great lady," Mildred Bliss, whose character informs every terrace and walkway. Since she got these two things right, the rest of the design is largely a matter of detail. Many fine gardens are composed *only* of a series of charming details—and how ultimately unsatisfying those places can feel! At Dumbarton Oaks, Mildred Bliss and her designers managed to transcend the decorative to create an unforgettable example of garden art.

This is the story of what Mildred Bliss did at Dumbarton Oaks, of how she did it, and of who helped her do it. It relies extensively on personal letters and previously unpublished reports and on the rich design documentation preserved in the Dumbarton Oaks archives, as well as on interviews with the few men and women who are still alive to tell the tale. Most important, the story is told in photographs taken at various times and in various seasons by the Thai photographer Ping Amranand. His exquisite images document the extraordinary beauty of the place.

Even after Mildred Bliss's death in 1967, Dumbarton Oaks continues to evolve. Like gardens everywhere, it is born again every spring.

Chapter One: 1920

At the back of a scholar's sketchbook is a painting—a watercolor fantasy of a nude in a garden. That titian-red hair; that pose—as if trying to wrap herself into some intricate yogic spinal twist; that look—calm but haughty, gazing off over one shoulder, cautious but in control: this is no seductive Venus lolling about in the shrubbery. There is no doubt about it—it is Mildred Bliss herself, delicate, demanding, generous, and vain; Mildred Bliss, the creator of Dumbarton Oaks, a unique center for scholarly research in Washington, D.C., which stands at the heart of one of the world's finest gardens. That garden was Mildred Bliss's passion: she dreamed it, she designed it, she paid for it, and for almost half a century, she steered it through its elaborate metamorphosis.

More than thirty years after Bliss's death, Dumbarton Oaks has the tenor not of a southern campus, which it is, but of a coolly formal New England prep school. The main gate leads from R Street, N.W., onto the South Lawn—a broad expanse of green fringed with specimen trees (a giant Katsura, deodar cedars, glossy-leafed Southern magnolias) and hidden from outside passersby with a high barrier of evergreen shrubs (mostly hollies and box). Above the drive, at the top of the hill, the stolid manse sits like a gem in its bezel. But in the back, behind the imposing facade, the garden opens up into a fantasy of invention.

Above:
Mildred Bliss in a watercolor from
Olaf Graybar's sketchbook,
"Vues de Dumbarton Oaks."

Looking down from the upper terrace is like taking the lid off a dollhouse. The garden is, in fact, a series of enclosed terraces and winding walkways—a "chambered nautilus of gardens," as someone once described it, because of the mysterious way the visitor is drawn from one space to the next. Unobtrusive exits off the various garden rooms lead down a flight of stairs or around a corner, where a flash of color, a fragrance, or a glinty pool is waiting.

Each space has its own character, and many serve distinct purposes. Next to the house sits the Star Garden, its paved floor design based on astrological symbols. This is an intimate outdoor room for dining. Every spring the Star is suffused with clouds of fragrant white azaleas. A short way down the hillside is the Ellipse walk, with its trim ariel hedge of pleached hornbeams (*Carpinus caroliniana*) surrounding a pool with an antique, carved stone fountain at its center. The Ellipse serves as a kind of promenade—the sinewy trunks of the hornbeams as graceful as a colonnade around its rim.

Still farther and slightly to the east is the Cutting Garden, where the flowers march along in no-nonsense rows. Positioned at one end of these utilitarian beds are stout toolsheds, like twin sentry towers. As self-contained as a small village, the estate's private, public, and working areas all comfortably coexist within the single, integrated whole of the garden.

Several principles have been adhered to since the plan was first laid out in the early 1920s. Full use is made of the trees already growing on the property and of native plants. Pruning has been kept minimal, with shrubs clipped to keep within certain boundaries but not shorn into unnatural forms. Near the house elements of the hardscaping—the built elements of a landscape design—are of carved Indiana limestone and brick. The degree of formality devolves as the terraces fall off down the steep hillside. Gradually the gardens become less prim and then almost wild, giving way to native stone and bluestone, and then to grassy paths. The result is that the garden feels as if it had always been there—born, not made.

Such was hardly the case. The garden at Dumbarton Oaks was developed with rigorous intensity between 1920 and 1965 under Mildred Bliss's scrupulous eye. Its romantic but inventive design is a reflection of her intrepid and disciplined character. "Dumbarton Oaks," states the British garden historian Jane Brown, "is a garden far, far superior to either Sissinghurst

Castle or Hidcote Manor in design, and it ranks (as they cannot) with the greatest gardens in the world, such as Villa d'Este or [Le Nôtre's] Vaux-le-Vicomte."

The same standards of excellence that Bliss demanded of the garden she required of herself. The watercolor sketch of a nude Bliss in a garden depicts her daily workout: the exercises referred to by everyone who visited Dumbarton Oaks simply as "Siposs." A yoga instructor from Austria, Herr Siposs was Mildred and Robert Bliss's "physical trainer," whom she had met while living in Argentina in the 1930s and imported back to Washington in 1933, along with a shipment of her most recently collected rare books and artifacts. Herr Siposs prescribed the Blisses' diet (fresh fruit for breakfast and dry, whole-wheat toast at lunch and dinner), as well as Mildred's physical training for the next fifteen years.

Guests at Dumbarton Oaks were not exempt from her routine. Mildred Bliss, Herr Siposs, the exercises, and the gardens were all described by a visiting British bird fancier, the historian Shane Leslie, in 1936 as "part of the unexpectedness of American life . . . I did not moon or meander while staying with the Blisses, for their Austrian instructor put me through physical exercises; and before I knew where I was Mrs. Bliss (though resembling a Chinese Tanagra) had picked me up and thrown me with the sheer strength of her little shoulders." The art historian Bernard Berenson described Mildred more succinctly, if with some slight sarcasm; he referred to her simply as "Perfect Bliss."

Not everyone would be so kind. Many of those who remember Mildred Bliss knew her in the 1960s when, at more than eighty years of age, she had become an imperious caricature of her former self. She was "a stern, wasp-waisted queen," Paul Richard, the art critic of the *Washington Post,* claimed, "with a whim of iron," according to her friend and Georgetown neighbor, the author Joseph Alsop. Little wonder that contemporary landscape historians by and large have critically dismissed her as a client who interfered as much as assisted with the work of professionals. Furthermore, they have implied that, when left to her own devices after 1946, Bliss destroyed the integrity of the initial landscape architect's design by arbitrarily reworking whole sections of the garden.

Yet the primary professional designer at Dumbarton Oaks, the American landscape gardener Beatrix Farrand, was particularly noted for adapting her designs to suit her clients' individual tastes. The garden was Farrand's poetic and exacting interpretation—in trees, shrubs, countless details—of Mildred Bliss's vision.

Bliss had visited grand estates abroad since her youth, when she had pasted snapshots of parterres and borders into her photograph album. By the age of forty-two, she was educated and discriminating, and (prior to Farrand's arrival) had a clear image of what should be done at Dumbarton Oaks. Yet although she began to devise her own planting schemes, she quickly realized that a professional was required. In 1922 she wrote: "It is the curse of a vivid imagination, with no training, to see the finished result and not know the means by which to obtain it. [But] I know exactly how every part of the place is going to look when it is done, even [down] to certain details."

Mildred Bliss participated as a full partner with Beatrix Farrand at every step of their more than thirty-year collaboration. She encouraged the landscape gardener to such an extent that, toward the end of her life, Beatrix Farrand would write, "There is no place that lies nearer to my heart than Dumbarton."

Farrand and Others

The same ability to locate and utilize the best talents was displayed in Bliss's work with other professionals on the property. She orchestrated the efforts of at least a half dozen designers at Dumbarton Oaks over a forty-five-year period. Dumbarton Oaks archivist James Carder's 1998 discovery of a set of overlooked drawings has brought to light the participation of French sculptor and decorator Armand Albert Rateau in the design work of the 1920s and 1930s. Bliss consulted with Rateau in Paris, and he visited Dumbarton Oaks in 1928. In his unpublished catalog of the Dumbarton Oaks garden hardscape elements, Carder has shown that Rateau helped conceptualize many of the built elements in the garden. Ideas expressed in Rateau's designs of 1929 were mined, modified, and brought to reality by Bliss and Farrand at Dumbarton Oaks over the next forty years.

By 1941 Beatrix Farrand had more or less stepped back from an active role at Dumbarton Oaks. Bliss, meanwhile, continued on with new schemes, enlisting the help of a drafter associated with Farrand's office, the architect Ruth Havey. The two women labored over the details of the hardscaping: railings, walkways, lanterns, and benches, all of which they submitted to Beatrix Farrand for her opinion, with Bliss having final approval.

Ruth Havey worked at Dumbarton Oaks through 1968. Long after 1940, when the property with its collections and libraries had been given to Harvard and changed from a private home to an educational institution, Bliss and Havey redesigned whole portions of the grounds, converting them to areas more suitable for public use. These new, more fanciful designs were closer to Mildred Bliss's ever-evolving taste. Ruth Havey was to work at Dumbarton Oaks intermittently for almost forty years, an association even longer than Beatrix Farrand's.

Bliss reworked areas of the garden into the 1960s. Her "big bang finale," as she put it, was to replace the old clay tennis courts near the house with an elegant and somewhat fantastic Italianate basin: the Pebble Pool. The pebbles formed the Bliss family crest: a wheat sheaf with the family motto of *Quod Severis Metes*—"As You Sow So Shall You Reap."

In terms of continuity of design, it is worth nothing that details of this last major addition to the garden—stacked-box columns, rocaille walls, flower-swagged urns, and Neptune figures—first appeared in a 1929 drawing by Armand Albert Rateau, one of a group of thirty-two that Rateau produced for Dumbarton Oaks. Elements from this very same drawing found their way into three different areas of the garden: in the swimming pool in 1931, in the Bosque in about 1932, and in the Pebble Pool in 1961.

Mildred Bliss never stopped. Astor Moore, the resident cabinetmaker at Dumbarton Oaks from 1964 to 1998, remembers that in her final years Bliss always scrutinized the garden with an eye toward making it better: "She was a Virgo, a perfectionist, like me . . . Some area in the garden would start to bother her and she'd say 'I need something for this space—do something.'" She and Moore would discuss the problem, and he would then make up a full-scale dummy of the bench or whatever it was they had decided to add. Bliss would live with the dummy in place in the garden for months, if necessary, fiddling with the details until a solution was reached. Only then was the final object installed.

Dumbarton Oaks became the repository of everything Mildred Bliss most loved: huge boxwoods, native woodland plants, carved stone quotations from Dante, reflective pools, classical ornament. It is a singular garden weighted with symbols and associations. To understand it, to see beyond its dazzling surface, it is necessary to understand something of its creator.

The Early Years of Mildred Bliss

On September 9, 1879, Mildred Barnes was born into one of the wealthiest families in America. Her father, Demas Barnes, a congressman from New York, was a geologist, writer, publisher, and educator, as well as one of the initial trustees of the Brooklyn Bridge and a lucky investor in Castoria patent medicine. ("Fletcher's Castoria" was a vegetable-based laxative for children that sold phenomenally for decades under the slogan "Children cry for it.") This particular investment was the source of the family fortune.

Demas Barnes died when Mildred was only nine years old. There was a scandal: her father's mistress initiated a court battle over the inheritance, but in the end Anna Dorinda Blakesley Barnes, Demas's second wife and Mildred's mother, inherited his substantial fortune.

With her marriage to Barnes the artistic Anna had become one of New York's celebrated "400," and she continued to live splendidly after his death. A spirited hostess and patron of the arts, she gave a half million dollars for the completion of Manhattan's new city hall, and when she moved to Montecito, California, she generously supported the local botanical garden and hospital.

Mildred, an only child, was very attached to her mother, who served as a lifelong model. Anna would also have another direct influence on her daughter's life. In the 1890s, she brought Mildred together with the two men who were to become pivotal to her daughter's future: Royall Tyler, the son of one of Anna's closest friends, and Robert Woods Bliss, the son of Anna's second husband. Tyler, her first love, encouraged Mildred's youthful interest in medieval art, collecting, and scholarship. He was to become the unseen hand behind the creation of Dumbarton Oaks. Robert Bliss, her gallant, protective stepbrother, was to become Mildred's devoted husband.

In 1897 Anna Barnes married again, to the widowed and prosperous St. Louis attorney William Henry Bliss. Vice president and general solicitor of the St. Paul and Duluth Railroad Co., and later associate counsel of the Northern Pacific Railroad, William Bliss had moved to Manhattan the year before they met. Upon his marriage to Anna, he promptly discontinued the practice of law.

Both Anna and William had children from previous marriages. Mildred Barnes was eighteen at the time of Anna's second marriage, and there was an older stepsister, Kora, from Demas Barnes's first marriage. William had both a twenty-two-year-old son, Robert, and a daughter, Annie Louise, close to Mildred in age.

Mildred had attended Miss Porter's School in Farmington, Connecticut. About the time of her mother's marriage, she went off to finishing school in Paris. Beautiful, curious, wealthy, and discriminating, Mildred had every opportunity before her. Anna's letters to her at this time were filled with a mother's earnest advice: which newspapers to read, which courses to pursue (singing lessons were strongly recommended). Furthermore, Anna asked that Mildred correspond in French and set forth lofty goals: "You will prove your birthright 'a noble woman, nobly planned' to help your fellow man and leave the world better for having been in it." Mildred was to "meet all the people of brains you can—good men and women—try to get them to talk and offer their views."

Top:
Mildred Barnes at four, with a pet dog.

Above:
Mildred Barnes as a young woman,
watercolor on ivory, c. 1895.

Top left:
Mildred Barnes at seven,
in a photograph that was always displayed
in her library.

Above left:
Mildred Barnes in the garden at the family
home in Sharon, Connecticut.

Top right:
Mildred Barnes and Robert Bliss at a
skating pond.

Above right:
Mildred Barnes and Robert Bliss with two
dogs, 1905.

Robert, meanwhile, attended Harvard College. An unenthusiastic student, he was petulant about his slim allowance but passionate about the arts, taking part in Hasty Pudding Club theatricals and attending the opera. While in Cambridge, Robert wrote to Mildred frequently, inviting her to football games and to the "Pudding dance": "Now don't please say you can't come, for I shall be broken if you do."

A petite redhead with porcelain skin and hazel eyes, Mildred was now twenty-two and just back from Paris. Robert, smitten by his stepsister, continuously teased, "Everyone who knows you thinks that you are about the nicest. But enough, I'll not say all the things people say of you for fear of your little head turning, although it is very level."

Scrapbooks and archives hold some clues to Mildred's youth. One scrapbook has a photograph of a seven-year-old Mildred playing the violin. As a relaxed and gregarious teenager she is shown hiking in the woods with friends; buttoned up in a white cotton dress and posed with a basket of lilies in front of the family home in Sharon, Connecticut; astride a horse in elegant riding attire; and glaring into the camera while tying up her ice skates as the dutiful Robert attends nearby.

Meanwhile Robert, after graduating from Harvard, signed on with the U.S. Foreign Service. Mildred must have sent some of the later photos to him when he was on his first posting in Puerto Rico, for he wrote back: "You've certainly been going a merry pace and I cannot say that I envy you in the least part of it, but I do the time you have in Sharon tramping about in the woods in the cold, crisp bracing air! . . . How those Kodaks carried me back . . ."

Another scrapbook features Mildred's newspaper clippings ("Unearthing the Sphinx") and sentimental poems. There are childish watercolors of a glass vase of purple and yellow pansies and of a dark pine forest (perhaps Mount Desert, Maine, where the family had a summer home); the published "Dress Regulations Approved by the Queen for Her Majesty's Drawing Rooms from the Lord Chamberlain's office, the Court of St. James"; and accounts detailing heroic acts by dogs ("The Dog That Died at His Post Rather Than Forsake a Dead Child").

One of the few relics from Mildred's early adulthood is entitled "A Catechism." Written when she was twenty-seven, in the year of her marriage, it provides insight into the ideas that would, fifteen years later, shape her concept for Dumbarton Oaks. Each chapter of the composition, an attempt to reconcile Christian doctrine with contemporary science, has a two-part, question-and-answer format:

Chapter I. Descent : Ancestry
Question: What are you?
Answer: I am a conscious human being upon earth and have become so by countless ages of development from the lowest form of life.

In later chapters the incipient humanist becomes clear:

Chapter V. Duty : Will : Character
Question: What is man's duty then?
Answer: His duty is to develop his better capacities to their utmost by helping his fellow men through understanding, justice and kindness, and to leave the "Grace" of his example behind him . . .
To inculcate a love of Beauty so true and so deep that passion, caprice and public opinion can never pervert it . . . should be the aim of all of us for each other and for ourselves . . .

Top:
Mildred Barnes, c. 1897.

Above:
Robert Bliss, c. 1897.

Accumulation is a danger, and the collecting of treasures a vain waste. To know, instead of to have, should be our rule . . . The French have a beautiful word, "Recueillment," which expresses . . . the idea of gathering of oneself into oneself for reflection. We should be able at will to close the outer portal and pray for that insight which alone leads towards wisdom, purity of motive and Godliness . . .
Failure comes out of our not living up to our own estimate of the best . . .

It was clear that Mildred Barnes had a sense of what she wanted her future to be: instilling knowledge and the love of beauty in others, living life generously, rigorously, and well. But just how she would accomplish this she had yet to determine.

Marriage

Mildred's future would be tied intimately to her past. Robert Bliss was made United States consul to Venice. He wrote Mildred long letters from abroad, and she, in turn, visited him at every assignment. In 1905 Robert wrote from Saint Petersburg in czarist Russia about the possibility of another foreign service job, a position "which I could hold and properly ask you to share with me . . . *you* know why." Three years later he was more frank: "You once asked me what I would do if you married another man," he wrote from Washington, D.C. "I wonder if I would have been . . . big enough to hide . . . the breaking of my heart." He then adds, "The President [Theodore Roosevelt] was *delighted* when I told him . . . of my approaching marriage and gave me most-hearty congratulations, I told him I was entitled to them in full measure."

It was during his assignment to Brussels in 1908 that Robert hastily returned to the United States and he and stepsister Mildred Barnes were wed. The ceremony took place on April 14 at Grace Church in Manhattan, "with no reception, save an informal one," according to the Brooklyn *Daily Eagle*. At the time the pairing was considered slightly scandalous: the wedding announcement in the *Baltimore Day* carried the headline "Weds His Father's Wife's Daughter." The bride was given away by her mother, and the union would last for fifty-four years.

The newlyweds returned to Robert's post in Belgium. They then made an occasion of the journey to Robert's next assignment—secretary of the legation in Buenos Aires—by sailing down the west coast of South America and at one point crossing the Andes by mule. Their stay in Buenos Aires coincided with the centennial of Argentine independence, a lengthy celebration that attracted a string of international visitors and exhibitions.

Tall, trustworthy Robert, with his elegant dress, perfect manners, and infectious humor, proved to be an ideal diplomatic representative. As a couple the Blisses were striking—engaged, intelligent, and at ease. But the emptiness of diplomatic functions and the "Babylonish existence," as Mildred put it, of life in Buenos Aires soon become apparent. Robert's subsequent assignment was to prove quite the opposite: in 1912 he was posted secretary of the embassy in Paris. Their experiences in France over the next seven years were to transform their lives.

Residing in Paris at that time was Royall Tyler, now a brilliant scholar and art historian. He and Mildred Bliss had shared some adventures of their own years before, in the 1890s, when their mothers had been close friends and had spent summers together with their children at the beach in Mattapoisette, Massachusetts.

Royall's mother, a widow, had remarried and moved with Royall and her new husband to Biarritz in 1900. In 1902, when Royall was eighteen and Mildred was just turning twenty-three, she and her mother visited their old friends in Italy. Following that visit, Royall began writing regularly to Mildred. Even in those first chatty letters, between comments about haircuts, Herodotus, *The Spectator,* and Tyrolean musicians, Royall advised Mildred on books to read and let her know of the treasures he had come across that she might wish to purchase for her collection.

Also in 1902, Royall entered Cambridge, and his incisive and irreverent chronicles captured her. Periodically he would disappear from school, once to wander through Spain with an aged monk, another time to travel to Rajputana in India ("a great country for sapphires"). And once Royall's stepfather asked him to convince the illustrious John Singer Sargent to do portraits of some family friends. All of these exploits were described in chatty, wry, "wicked" letters that Mildred would save for the rest of her life.

Mildred fell in love with Royall (perhaps Robert was thinking of him in his comments about Mildred possibly marrying someone else); in 1904 she even had their horoscopes compared by an astrologer. The astrologer, Professor St. Leon of New York City, advised against the marriage: "[Royall's] sun is in conjunction with her Mars, and this would eventually bring a conflict . . . in which I fear he would not be charitable enough to allow her the right of her opinions."

Too opinionated to be dissuaded by mere star charts, she and Royall were planning a tour together through Spain as late as March 1908: Mildred was to arrive in Gibraltar on April 7. Royall eagerly wrote that she should be sure to pack a black dress, "preferably dirty and tattered," for he would be taking her to places where even Spanish women were rarely seen. Then, suddenly, inexplicably, Mildred decided not to go.

There are two plausible reasons. In his last letter to Mildred before the trip, dated March 7, Royall had made it clear that he was in Europe to stay. He commented that whereas Mildred had in her last letter described America as "amazing," he felt that the "high degree of its amazingness [is] not enough to make one want to spend one's life there. Europe is still amazinger along most lines that interest me." If Mildred had been thinking of marriage to Royall, that would have meant spending the rest of her life in foreign lands, a step that she perhaps was not ready to take. Another reason for Mildred's sudden change of heart may have been that she had gotten wind of Royall's growing interest in his publisher's wife, Elisina, a beautiful Florentine princess— although the precise date that marks the beginning of that liaison is cloudy.

In any event, Mildred abruptly canceled the trip in mid-March and married Robert Bliss less than one month later. She invited Royall to visit the couple at Robert's post in Brussels, but he responded that he could not come: he had too much to do.

The astrologer had foreseen much else for Mildred's future. Sixteen pages of charts and advice included the following observations:

She will inherit money, by the wills and legacies of the dead, but it will require a great deal of tact and skill to hold on to it . . . Her husband will be a person of good family and position, very much attached to the native . . . The native is very popular with the opposite sex. She will have many strong friends, and will mix with strange or eccentric people . . . She has Oriental tastes and there are indications of journeys into foreign lands during the course of her life . . . The native will pass through some very uncommon ordeals, yet her life will be more fortunate than otherwise & she will have a very successful ending.

It was not until 1910 that Royall confided in Mildred (then still in Buenos Aires) of Elisina and their plans to marry—a difficult situation, since Elisina was already married to Royall's editor and had four children. Mildred did not hesitate to wish the two lovers well. To Royall she wrote: "The 'usual formulas' do not serve me . . . There is no need to try to explain Love. It *is*—and it is only in the attainment of the peace that comes of it, that means differ . . . If you both find the happiness I want for you, the wisdom of yr. coming together will be proved."

In an attached letter to the now-pregnant Elisina, Mildred was unusually candid: "I am still waiting and longing for a child . . . I wish I could talk with you. It would be a great refreshment in the bustling stagnation and crowded solitude of the intolerably superficial existence our 'career' obliges us to lead . . . I pray constantly for the strength to hold my inner self intact."

The Blisses never were to have children of their own, although it could be said that Dumbarton Oaks became something of a substitute. They did, however, become godparents of Royall and Elisina's new baby, William Tyler, who grew up to become, among other things, the second director of the Dumbarton Oaks Study and Research Center.

Mildred's comments to Royall, when she was asked to become William's godmother, illustrate her indifference to the "usual formulas":

Although I was baptised by three Protestant denominations(!) I have never been confirmed into any church. Several times I have been to the communion table . . . but it occasioned controversy . . . in each case the clergymen, when informed of my unorthodoxy, admitted me on the personal ground of Deism, right living and with the hope of confirmation.

Paris 1912

On April 20, 1912, the Blisses set sail from New York for France and Robert's new post. Five days later they were in Paris and dining with Royall Tyler. Mildred's engagement book indicates that she and Robert lunched with both Royall and Elisina soon after, and then Mildred went to the ballet, to the Louvre (with Royall), and to meet Edith Wharton, the American author, for tea. Mildred undoubtedly had read Wharton's novels, as well as her influential articles on interior decoration and Italian gardens.

Edith Wharton was an important person for Mildred to get to know. She was a respected artist, well placed socially and financially, and at the center of the American expatriate artistic community in Europe. She knew many of the people Mildred would want to befriend, and her opinion mattered; in fact, in many ways Wharton was to become Bliss's model. As Mildred had done with her mother, she and Wharton henceforth corresponded with one another solely in French. Bliss admitted to her admiration for the author following Wharton's death in 1937, writing that Edith had been her "stimulus for nearly forty years."

Worldly diplomats, Europeanized Americans, writers, painters, musicians—all considered Paris their spiritual home. Soon after the Blisses' arrival Mildred entered into the city's artistic life, having met more than a few of its leading luminaries, such as the Polish pianist Paderewski, at her mother's salon back in America. "2 Paderewskis" were at a dinner, Mildred noted in her engagement book on August 6, and "Paddy played!"

Robert, too, fell in with the general excitement. "Soon after reaching Paris," Robert told a reporter in 1958, "my old and dear friend Royall Tyler . . . took me to the little shop of an antique dealer on the Boulevard Raspail, Joseph Brummer, who had some material from Peru. I had never seen anything like it and I bought . . . an Olmec jadite figure. That was the beginning. That day the collector's microbe took root in—it must be confessed—very fertile soil. Thus in 1912 were sewn the seeds of an incurable malady!" Robert Bliss, the trusty diplomat and lover of opera, was now transformed into a passionate collector of the sensual and symbol-laden art of the early South American cultures.

Under similar tutelage from Royall and from the connoisseur Bernard Berenson as well, Mildred developed her own interest in early Christian, or Byzantine, art. Berenson, a native of Boston, had studied at Harvard and was briefly mentored by Isabella Stewart Gardner. Interestingly, Berenson, Gardner, and Edith Wharton all took classes at Harvard with influential art historian Charles Eliot Norton. From 1896 to 1900, Berenson had helped Gardner assemble one of the finest private collections of Old Master paintings and objects. These were installed in a transported Italian palazzo, Fenway Court, in Boston, which served as Gardner's home until she died in 1924, bequeathing it to Boston as a museum.

The simple accumulation of objects, as Mildred had written in her catechism, was never her goal, so in addition to old pieces of silver, bone, and textile, the Blisses began to assemble a library that included rare books and manuscripts, seeking to broaden their understanding of these complex subjects. Attractive and personable, fluent in Italian, German, French, Spanish, and Portuguese, "extraordinarily interested in all aspects of life," according to one friend, Mildred Bliss became the consummate diplomat's wife. Wrote an observer in Paris at the time: "[Mildred] was also the brains of the whole Embassy." Mildred, thoroughly at ease, described her new life to a friend: "Paris whirls by and through us—a potpourri of . . . tangos, balls, dinners, Ballets Russes . . ."

War

But the charmed world that was Paris in 1912 did not last. In the late summer of 1914 World War I began. It was assumed that the war would be short in duration—perhaps only a few weeks. Nevertheless, in those first months the Blisses privately donated six ambulances to the French (they eventually donated a total of twenty-three ambulances and three staff cars), and they established a war relief charity, Comité des Enfants de la Frontière, eventually opening some thirty-three shelters to house and educate the orphans of war-torn Europe.

Throughout the war, Mildred Bliss poured what emerged as considerable organizational skills into fund-raising and promotion for many charities: American Distributing Service, American Red Cross, National American Committee of the Polish Victims Relief Fund, Voluntary Aid Detachment (British), Oeuvres des Maisons Américaines des Convalescence (French), Aide des Artistes (French), Formations Chirurgicales Mobiles Franco-Russes (international), and others. Such duties were obligatory for women of Bliss's social class. Edith Wharton, with her deep patrician roots, and Bliss—both formidable characters—inevitably found themselves working together closely, sometimes contentiously, on numerous wartime projects.

A subtle rivalry developed, more openly expressed by Wharton than by Bliss, who even at the worst of times always retained an attitude of admiration, even awe, for the author. After an especially trying meeting, Wharton confided to Elisina Tyler, "I seem to poison [Mildred] after I've been with her for half an hour and she gets perfectly horrid." Wharton set up two private civilian charities herself at the start of World War I, and Royall and Elisina Tyler administered the charities for her throughout the conflict.

As World War I extended from weeks into years, the Blisses' frustrations were compounded. Even at the worst of times, however, Mildred maintained an amazing range of activities—petitioning on behalf of friends in need, overseeing charities, organizing events (including, with Edith Wharton, a series of concerts to benefit needy musicians), even traveling, all the while still managing to make time for cultural respites—as an impressionistic letter dated August 24, 1916, makes clear. Mildred, in despair at the news of the British defeat at Jutland, wrote: "The end of the world seemed clearly to have arrived, and with one's last confidence shaken . . . there did not seem any use in trying to go on fighting it out . . ." But in everyday life she found "a few bright spots . . . and one of them was an hour of primitive [early] music at the Sainte Chapelle . . . On the whole it's all so sad . . . There is not one word or a look or a fact in the whole day that is not in some indirect way scarred by this iniquitous war; and yet I wouldn't—if I could, be anywhere else in this wide world—save just here in France . . . for I know somehow that one is living the best now."

The intensity of life created permanent bonds. "I have grown to care so much for Paris and for certain friends," she wrote in the last days of the war. "I can't imagine ever living away for long—Oh! there goes a cannon."

And unlike her "intolerably superficial existence" in Argentina, Paris had become Bliss's proving ground as well as her home. Living through the chaos of World War I while overseeing her various causes and charities left Mildred confident of her abilities: she could manage anything, she realized, and under the very worst of circumstances. Mildred's modus operandi, which would serve her so well in later life, was simple: she found talented, like-minded individuals upon whom she could rely to organize the mundane day-to-day elements of each project.

Years later William Tyler offered a very different perspective on Mildred in wartime; Tyler recalled a time in 1916 when he was six:

Mr. and Mrs. Bliss came to stay, and I was awed by her: a vision of elegance and mystery, with furs, a large hat, long gloves and exotic perfume, who swooped down on me and asked me if I would like to see her do a fox trot. Confused by this abracadabra, I merely hung my head, whereupon this vision turned on its heels and started taking short jerky steps with little turns around the room, holding its arms half extended before it. I suffered extreme embarrassment from all this, but the present of a silver pen-knife, my first, restored my composure.

Above:
Anna Dorinda Blakesley Barnes Bliss,
Mildred's mother and Robert's stepmother.

Opposite top:
Mildred Bliss upon being named a
Chevalier of the Legion d'Honneur.

Opposite bottom:
Robert Bliss, c. 1919.

Back in America, Anna and William Bliss had discovered the beauty of California and would soon purchase property in Montecito. In 1918 Anna Bliss built a magnificent sixty-five-room mansion with forty-eight acres of gardens, the Casa Dorinda. There, a local newspaper reported, the guest list came to include King Albert and Queen Elizabeth of Belgium (who planted a sequoia on the lawn in 1919); President Herbert Hoover; and musicians Ignacy Paderewski (who found the Casa Dorinda "the most agreeable and enjoyable private house in which I played in America . . . it was like celebrating a mass") and Jascha Heifetz. The reporter wrote: "Mrs. Bliss's bedroom was connected by a corridor which appears in perspective to be a mile and a furlong in length . . . and this hallway was known as the 'Corridor of Delights.'" Delights notwithstanding, William Bliss, "tiring of his wife's insatiable propensity for entertaining, soon packed his bags and moved with his valet into a house in Santa Barbara for the duration of his marriage." The Casa Dorinda itself would be sold after Anna Bliss's death (and is now a retirement home).

In 1917 the United States finally entered the war. Robert Bliss, thoroughly enmeshed in the politics, remained steadfastly at the embassy in Paris through changes in ambassador until the peace treaty was signed in November 1918. Robert and Mildred Bliss then stayed on in Europe for another several months while Robert acted as the United States representative to the peace conference in Brussels. Both Blisses received innumerable honors for their wartime activities. Mildred was decorated for her charitable activities by Belgium, Greece, and Britain. Mildred and Robert, Edith Wharton, and Royall and Elisina Tyler each received France's highest civilian award, presented by the president of France: Chevalier of the Legion d'Honneur.

A Home Base in America

In the fall of 1919 the Blisses returned to America. After nineteen years in the foreign service, seven of which were in France, and with only occasional visits back to the United States, Robert Bliss was ready for a change: "On the steamer from France I said to my wife that we had been away for too long, and that I felt we must put roots into our own land."

At the time of their departure, Wharton wrote that she had heard Mildred was "looking poorly" and Robert "convalescent." (Both Blisses suffered from frequent bouts of poor health.) Several months at the Casa Dorinda in sunny California restored them, at least temporarily. April 1920 found the Blisses in Washington, D.C., with Robert appointed chief of the Division of Western European Affairs at the Department of State. Robert's collection of pre-Columbian artifacts, Mildred's Byzantine treasures, their books, and their household objects—all had grown to proportions impossible to cart about from one diplomatic posting to the next. "It had always been my dream to live in a country place in the city," Robert once said, "and so I started looking around the District of Columbia. A property called 'the Oaks' was suggested . . . and though it had no particular charm and the grounds were unkempt and in places much overgrown, the beautiful trees gave promise of possibilities to a gardener." Sensitive to Mildred's love of gardens, Robert hoped that the sylvan setting might engage her. For his part, The Oaks, located on the highest point in Georgetown and bordering Rock Creek Park, was rural in feel yet located less than two miles from the White House. It seemed perfect to him.

To Mildred Bliss, however, the situation was less than ideal. In June 1920, just nine months after they had returned to the United States, she was eagerly making a first trip back to her beloved Paris. Robert wrote to her aboard ship:

I can sense the emotions which dominate you as France looms on the horizon . . . that the moment of return to the life and friends you love has arrived [and] your pent up feeling will need watching. In the long run of a lifetime both a man and a woman should establish a solid base and a proper background,—and I know that I am right in wanting them in my own country; in a foreign one it would not be a success—and even for you, with all of your charm, beauty and intelligence—you would be ever a foreigner and a foreigner cannot overcome completely the fact that he is an outsider.
Look at Edith [Wharton]—not that I compare you to her—God forbid!

Robert had met with the owner of The Oaks to discuss the details of the purchase, and he added:

Did you get my cable about the Oaks, and are you as excited and thrilled as I am? . . . This really is a lovely place and I will revel in it. The old house can be made a dream of loveliness, while the grounds have infinite possibilities. Perhaps you may want to return earlier than in Sept. just to look at it again. All summer long I will be thinking of nothing else, and politics can go bang!

That Mildred Bliss fled at the idea of living in America, let alone Washington, D.C., then a sleepy, provincial southern town, is not surprising; besides, all of her friends were in Europe. She went to France in 1920 with the hope of finding a "more suitable" Parisian apartment than the one that she and Robert already owned—to establish her own "home base" in the city she had grown to love above all others. "By more suitable," says Dumbarton Oaks archivist James Carder, "she meant more *grand.* I would imagine that The Oaks, with its dilapidated wraparound porches and Victorian turrets, must have appeared to her a nightmare."

The Oaks of Georgetown

The Oaks had originally been granted by Queen Anne to the Scotsman Col. Ninian Beall in 1702. Beall named any number of his Maryland properties after places in his native land, and he named this mount the Rock of Dumbarton after a castle on the River Clyde near his Highland home. By 1712, 795 acres of the land, including the Rock of Dumbarton, were offered for sale for 168 pounds sterling. The sale did not go through, and Beall ended up leaving the property to his son, George. (The name Georgetown was probably in honor of King George III, but it was sometimes said that "George Town," as it was first called, was a name referring to George Beall and George Gordon, both major landholders and the first people to settle in the area.)

George Beall willed the property to his two sons, and it was one of these, Colonel George Beall, who began to farm the land. By 1798, the estate, divided between the now wealthy brothers and reduced by further sales, consisted of only eighty acres.

Above:
Dumbarton Oaks, then known as Monterey, c. 1860, with Robert Beverley's elegant new Orangery.

The land speculator, lawyer, and politician William "Pretty Billy" Hammond Dorsey purchased the house and just twenty acres for two thousand pounds in 1800. In 1801 he built a two-story Federal-style house within the oak grove at the top of the hill. His family moved into the handsome brick dwelling that year, but losses from land speculation forced Dorsey to sell the property within four years. Robert Beverley purchased the estate for $1,500. Engaged in banking and shipping, Beverley, who had been schooled at Cambridge, renamed the property Acrolophos (Grove on the Hill) in 1805 and added the elegant brick-and-glass orangery pavilion that still stands to the east of the house.

The widow Colhoun (later changed to Calhoun) became the estate's next owner; her late husband had purchased Acrolophos from Beverley for ten thousand dollars in 1823. She deeded the property to her son-in-law, James, who soon allowed his brother-in-law John C. Calhoun of South Carolina, secretary of war and later vice president to John Quincy Adams, to move into Acrolophos, which John Calhoun promptly renamed Oakly. Unfortunately Oakly proved so expensive to maintain that, within a year, John Calhoun moved out and put the estate up for rent. In 1828 he wrote, "The property is going to waste." That year Oakly was sold for eight thousand dollars to Brooke Mackall of Georgetown.

Mackall worked for the United States Treasury in the customs service. For seventeen years Mackall, his wife, and their children—five of whom were born in the house—lived at Oakly, until the combined economic blows of the death of his father and the loss of his government job forced the sale of the property.

Edward Linthicum, a hardware store dealer and part owner of several ships, purchased the house plus twenty-two acres in 1846 for $11,500. Linthicum gradually enlarged the house, transforming Oakly into "the showplace of the

District" with "a well-filled greenhouse, flower gardens on the east, wooded lawn in front, grove of forest trees on the west, and gently sloping and well-sodded hills to the south, all of which were kept in perfect order," according to a Georgetown neighbor.

Linthicum first rechristened Oakly Monterey, after the battle in the war with Mexico in which his son-in-law had been killed, but by 1860 called the property The Oaks after the magnificent trees that lent such dignity to the property (the aged trees, British visitor Shane Lesley surmised later, "must have remembered British allegiance"); some of those trees are still standing. The Oaks eventually passed on to Linthicum's widow's grandson, Edward Linthicum Dent, who died at the age of thirty-nine in 1899; before he died he divided and sold off much of the property.

In 1891 the estate, with six acres of land, was acquired for $105,000 by Col. Henry Fitch Blount, who also managed to buy back much of the former acreage. The well-traveled and sociable Blount family moved into the house at The Oaks, and their pet peacock, Pico, patrolled the grounds. (Pico may have been alive when the Blisses purchased the property; decades later friends would occasionally affectionately address Mildred as "Pico.") But by 1920, only Blount's widow remained in residence.

Robert Bliss wanted to see himself and his wife settled, with a home base in the United States. As he saw it, the requirements were simple: he desired a "country place in the city," while Mildred wanted grounds that could be turned into the kind of thing they were familiar with from their friends' estates in Europe. In a *Washington Star* article published in 1956, Robert mentioned two specific features that drew him to the house. One was the flight of stairs at each end of the north gallery (according to the *Star*, he was "tired of houses where the staircase hit you in the eyes as you entered"). The second feature was Beverley's elegant Orangery on the building's east side, "with its *ficus ripens*, a close-clinging vine, covering the walls." The creeping fig (*Ficus pumila* in today's taxonomy) is a small-leafed, slow-growing vine, and still covers the walls of the Orangery, the most beautiful of all the rooms at The Oaks.

Historian Walter Muir Whitehead maintained that it was not the house at all that attracted the Blisses but a "superb location and the fine trees and charming variety of topographical contours." At The Oaks the land drops approximately one hundred feet from the rise on which the house sits to a creek some six hundred feet to the north. The preexisting, albeit rudimentary, terracing of this steep slope could not fail to have suggested to Mildred Bliss the siting of many of the great Italian country houses of the sixteenth through the eighteenth centuries. (She was familiar with such Renaissance villas both from her travels in Italy and from Edith Wharton's influential *Italian Villas and Their Gardens* of 1919.)

Recalling the property when she first laid eyes on it in 1921, Beatrix Farrand noted that "before alterations were made the house was a solid, ugly, brick construction [but] surrounded by magnificent oaks and placed far enough back from the adjoining streets of Georgetown to still keep a semi-rural air." In other words, with work The Oaks had the potential to become exactly what Mildred and Robert each desired.

"Arrd. Paris 1 A.M.," Mildred jotted in her engagement book on June 6, 1920. In a letter of the same date, back in Washington, Robert wrote to her that the widow of Henry Blount "is an old dear, but not a fool." Robert offered $125,000 for the property "and she came down to $150." Even then the sale was not entirely smooth. Robert wrote again two days later at midnight:

Right:
The earliest known photograph of Dumbarton Oaks, then named Oakly, pre-1860.

Below right:
The south (front) facade, c. 1890, Victorianized with additional porches and a new roofline.

Bottom right:
The Oaks's north facade and barn (later removed), c. 1900.

There is a slight hitch with the settlement on the Oaks sale . . . I am so keen to have the matter determined, and the papers signed, so that I can begin making plans. It will be an ideal house for you and me, and we will be happy there, I know, for it is a good frame for you, my Blessed Angel. I miss you frightfully . . .

The "slight hitch"—the difference in price—was resolved, and The Oaks was purchased on October 15. Robert Bliss later said: "After we had bought the place many of my friends said I was crazy to think of settling in Georgetown, where no one would take the trouble to go . . . That was in 1920!"

Everyone knew everyone else in the Blisses' circle. They traveled to the same destinations, attended the same parties, read the same books, visited one another's houses, shared garden tips, architects, and gossip. Transforming The Oaks would not be so very different from what the Blisses had seen their friends doing abroad. In Italy Bernard Berenson at the Villa I Tatti and Sir Harold Acton at La Pietra had renovated centuries-old villas, creating elaborate Italian Renaissance–style gardens on the estates. In England the American Lawrence Johnston was creating his own innovative variations on Italianate garden rooms at Hidcote Manor. And very soon Edith Wharton, both outside of Paris at the Pavillon Colombe and in the south of France in a converted convent at Hyères, would be busy creating new gardens of her own—twenty-two terraces of them. Comments about the plantings at La Colombe were soon to fill Wharton's letters.

That summer Mildred Bliss did not find a "more suitable" place, but she did reestablish a home away from home in Paris in her former apartment on the rue Henri Moisson—conducting something of a full-scale renovation project. But she also began making purchases for the new house in Washington. (Her mother had advised before her departure: "Are you going to Italy this trip? Mme. Lindsay writes from Florence the beautiful & blessed & wonderfully historic—that the antiques shops are filled with requisite old objects d'art—finer than Rome.")

Mildred returned from Europe on September 1 and was "flat" for a week. But apparently she had made up her mind to tackle the neglected estate. Transforming The Oaks, she decided, could become a new focus for her creative energies. The gardens were to prove so seductive, in fact, that they became Mildred Bliss's ruling passion for the next forty-five years.

The Transformation Begins

When Mildred Bliss returned to the United States, she used memories of civilized life in Europe before the war as the model for the home she planned to create. In those grand Edwardian estates, as at her mother's new home at the Casa Dorinda, a music room, libraries, artworks, and beautifully landscaped gardens were de rigueur. Bliss determined that the overall scheme for the gardens at The Oaks would be based on the Mediterranean model, first developed by the Romans, in which the outdoor spaces, and especially those areas nearest the house, are treated as rooms—extensions of the interior living areas.

The steep slope at The Oaks suggested an organization along the lines of Italian Renaissance gardens, with the individual garden rooms dropping down the hillside in terraces, their character gradually devolving from formal and architectural near the house to informal and naturalistic at the perimeter. There would be a loggia, shady arbors, small amphitheater, *giardino segreto*, and commanding views from the upper terraces—all very Italian. But for the finishing details, which were largely designed from the mid-1930s on, Bliss, who gradually became a true Francophile under the influence of Edith Wharton and of the American artist and collector Walter Gay and his wife, styled the gardens in the French manner, with every element specifically designed and perfectly proportioned for its space and purpose.

The architect Frederick H. Brooke began renovations to The Oaks in 1920, a process that entailed ripping off the many nineteenth-century embellishments that obscured the simple lines of the original Federal shell and removing layers of battleship-gray paint from the exterior to restore the original color of the hand-fired bricks. (According to Robert Bliss, those bricks probably came from Holland or England as sailing-ship ballast.) Within one week of her return from France, Mildred Bliss began meeting with Brooke at least once a week.

She began the landscaping by repositioning the enormous box bushes that the former owner, Henry Blount's widow, had regularly purchased and carted home as nearby Georgetown properties went up for sale. By November 1920, Bliss had made several visits to the United States National Arboretum, which still serves as a living encyclopedia of what flourishes in the Washington region. But before too long, she realized that the combined tasks of taking care of both house and grounds were on a scale beyond what she alone could handle.

The Philadelphia metalsmith Samuel Yellin was brought in, in May 1921, to design a number of ornaments for the house. In the main hall he created two three-story wrought-iron stair railings that are fantasies of leaves, branches, birds, and small animals native to the region. For the exterior, he fabricated a series of decorative rainwater scuppers, as well as wrought-iron railings and window grilles. One of those railings, installed along a short flight of steps connecting the house to the Orangery, features iron rings for flower pots along its outer side.

Long before Yellin had arrived at The Oaks—in fact, twenty-five years earlier, in 1896—Mildred's mother had given a young landscape gardener her first professional assignment: to drain a swampy area on the family's property in Bar Harbor, on Mount Desert, Maine. That young designer was Edith Wharton's niece, Beatrix Cadwallader Jones (later Farrand). She was just seven years older than Mildred.

In January 1921, Mildred Bliss invited Beatrix Jones Farrand to Washington to visit the Georgetown property. Bliss may have worn a French couture suit, while Farrand was probably garbed in serviceable Irish tweeds, her usual traveling outfit. Nevertheless, the two women had a great deal in common: similar backgrounds, similar tastes, many of the same friends.

If Bliss harbored any lingering doubts about the undertaking, they must have disappeared when Elisina Tyler wrote that, at Hyères, Edith Wharton had succeeded in making "a charming house out of a rather desolate-looking prieure." Mildred Bliss must have viewed her own attempt at making a "charming house" out of The Oaks as a similar undertaking. The competitive adrenaline unleashed, she launched wholeheartedly into the renovations.

Above:
Samuel Yellin, charcoal study for
an unrealized iron grille with wheat sheaf
design, c. 1921.

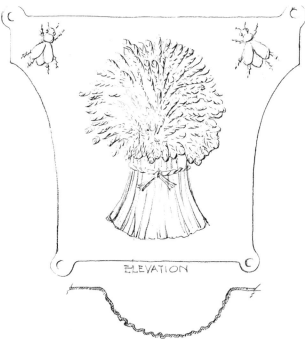

ELEVATION

Above:
North Vista, c. 1920, as Mildred Bliss
oversaw the repositioning of the boxwood.

Left:
Samuel Yellin, design for a decorative rain
scupper with bee and wheat sheaf motif,
c. 1921.

Chapter Two: 1921–1922

Tuesday, January 25, 1921, was to be a moderately busy day in Mildred Bliss's life: seven appointments, two of them before noon. One of those morning meetings, noted in pencil in Bliss's loose hand, indicates the first meeting between Beatrix Farrand and Mildred Bliss specific to Dumbarton Oaks. Bliss had invited the landscape gardener to come to Washington, D.C., and look over the estate. Winter was a good time for this purpose: the trees were bare, the shape of the land unobscured by vegetation. By summoning Beatrix Farrand, Mildred Bliss was committing herself to a full redesign of the property. But it is unlikely, at that moment, that she could foresee all that this would encompass: it would entail not simply the creation of an elaborate garden but the initiation of a more than forty-year-long project, as well as the start of an intense and complex friendship.

Farrand at the time was busy juggling a variety of landscaping jobs: two small, informal projects on Mount Desert; a suite of traditional gardens for Adele and Otto H. Kahn and an elaborate Chinese-style rock garden for Harrison Williams, both on Long Island; and institutional work at college campuses in New Jersey and Ohio. She sandwiched her visit to Washington into one of her circuits of ongoing projects, a closely packed schedule that regularly took her from Maine to New York to points south and back again.

How did Beatrix Farrand come to be Mildred Bliss's choice? Anna Bliss's early connection to the landscape gardener, combined with the fact that Edith Wharton had probably spoken of her niece to Bliss in Paris, probably set the course. In any event, Beatrix Farrand's work could easily have come to Mildred Bliss's attention on its own, since the designer was already twenty-five years into her professional career: Farrand had completed some eighty projects by 1921. She was the choice of any number of East Coast clients on a social par with the Blisses, among them Mrs. Woodrow Wilson, John D. Rockefeller, and Edward S. Harkness. In 1916 Farrand's plan for the Rose Garden at the White House had been implemented, and three years later she had designed the memorial stone for Theodore Roosevelt.

Archivist James Carder has observed that the majority of the artists and architects who worked with Mildred Bliss at Dumbarton Oaks were the children of family friends or had other social connections with the Blisses. This pattern must have provided Bliss with a resonant context as well as with the expediency of working with people of similar backgrounds.

And so, Bliss asked Farrand to visit The Oaks within six months of its purchase. Farrand's second visit came eight months later, in August, to meet with Bliss and the rest of her team: the architect Frederick Brooke and the metalworker Samuel Yellin.

Mildred Bliss's ideas for the garden began well before she brought a professional onto the scene. The British landscape architect Lanning Roper, a friend to both Bliss and Farrand, has stated that "Mrs. Bliss knew from the start what she wanted to create. She had definite conceptions, some of which she had treasured from childhood. Others were inspired by her varied travels, for she loved to [adopt] ideas, designs and even actual details of ornament and architecture . . . to the [special] needs of Dumbarton Oaks." The eighteenth-century cast-lead sculptures on the Fountain Terrace, the beautiful Provençal carved stone fountain in the Ellipse, the decorative urns, and the rose-pink marble benches are all treasures that Bliss gathered in Europe and shipped back to The Oaks. Roper continues:

Certain basic principles were laid down for Mrs. Farrand. As Dumbarton Oaks was going to be a permanent town residence there must be year-round interest with a predominance of evergreens, both coniferous and broad-leaved . . . the flowers ... were to be carefully chosen for color and form to enhance the scheme but ... never to dominate it. Furthermore certain sections of the garden were to be entirely green, with ground covers chosen for contrasting leaf forms, colors and textures ... Her charming conception of trees planted to form a high arched alley, feathery backgrounds, reflecting pools and winding paths started in childhood as an idée fixe ...

The silver-maple canopy of Mélisande's Allée leading to the sylvan Lovers Lane (or Theater) Pool are the areas of the garden that best express this childhood vision. Roper also noted:

Because of the dramatic slope of the site, it was obvious that the garden must consist of a series of broad terraces leading from the strictly formal architectural character of the house through various transitions to the delightful informality of the lower garden ... Lastly, Mrs. Bliss wished to incorporate in the garden a wealth of ornament executed in a variety of media to illustrate the wide range of decorative architectural detail and ornament available.

Mildred Bliss's love of ornament and symbol led her to use allusive names and quotations throughout the garden. The name "Mélisande" in "Mélisande's Allée," for example, refers to the character in Maurice Maeterlinck's play, which was the basis for the seminal opera by Claude Debussy. *Pelléas et Mélisande* premiered in Paris in 1902 and was seen by Royall Tyler, who wrote enthusiastically about seeing it to Mildred in 1905. Mélisande's Allée likely refers to a sylvan setting from the play.

Although much of the hardscaping detail was completed by Bliss's work with Ruth Havey after about 1933, Bliss and Farrand did design some significant hardscaping in the garden. Mildred Bliss made her requirements clear to Beatrix Farrand from the start, for there is an attention to detail in the hardscaping and a perfection in its execution that runs consistently through the garden's almost fifty-year development.

Mildred Bliss kept up her weekly meetings with the architect Frederick Brooke through the spring. But in mid-May she left again for France. Six days later she was lunching in Paris with Edith Wharton, each, no doubt, describing plans for their new gardens. When she got back to Washington, four months later, Bliss set to work on The Oaks with renewed vigor, meeting with Brooke about every other day.

She was always on the lookout for suggestions. That spring she wrote to Frank Chapman of New York's Museum of Natural History: "I need a bit of advice as to how to attract birds. Our place in Georgetown ought to be a haven for all sorts of permanent and migratory birds, and we want as large an orchestra as we can get."

The impressions of Beatrix Farrand during this period of initial work are summarized in a letter of July 7, 1922. Her characteristic Yankee reserve was lifted somewhat by the realization that, on her visit, she had left behind her fountain pen, foot rule, and other "impedimenta":

I do not really usually behave as badly as this and do not display my pin-headedness so obviously ... It may sound ungracious to say I am glad to delay beginning work on the Oaks for a couple of months [Farrand was about to sail to France for two months] ... You have no idea of the feeling I have always had for your people on account of my first work having come to me from your family ... What I shall try and do with the Oaks is to simply be your gardening pair of hands, carrying out your ideas. As our minds run along the same lines it is going to be quite exciting to see when we think

Above:
Beatrix Cadwallader Jones, c. 1890.

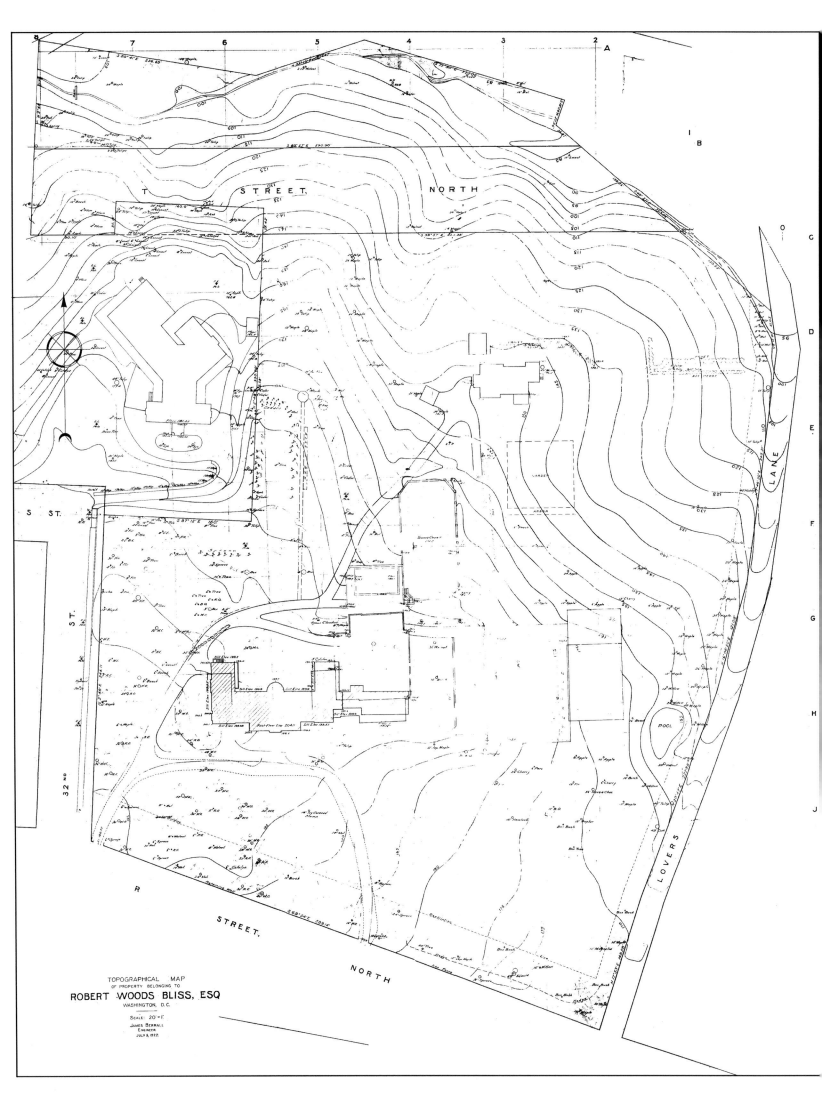

TOPOGRAPHICAL MAP
OF PROPERTY BELONGING TO
ROBERT WOODS BLISS, ESQ
WASHINGTON, D. C.

SCALE: 20' = 1'

JAMES BERRALL
ENGINEER.
JULY 8, 1922.

*simultaneously the same ideas and I shall look for sharp criticism from you—
and shall equally tell you if your ideas do not seem to me likely to work well.*

Opposite:
Topographical survey of The Oaks,
July 5, 1922.

The Landscaping Plan of 1922

Farrand continued in her letter with a reference to a topographical survey of
The Oaks, dated July 5, 1922, which had been prepared at her suggestion. "The
fall of the land between the end of the Orangery and the water level of the pool
is incredible. There is a drop of over forty feet which makes the terraces quite
an amusing study . . . you may be quite sure that I will take my survey with
me and fuss over it happily on my journeys . . ." Five pages of lists of perennial
flower seeds, summer flower seeds, and plants for the garden were attached.

Farrand then enclosed an exuberant seven-page overview of her impressions.
This report is of special interest for two reasons: it reveals how immediately
sympathetic she was to Bliss's vision for the gardens; and it records how
many of Bliss's initial ideas were, in fact, primary to the design of The Oaks:

*The Oaks offers opportunities for development on so many different lines that
it is difficult to know which to emphasize most strongly in the beginning . . .*

*It would seem as though the whole street front section of the place should be
treated from the point of view of some of the large, ample, old, half-city/
half-country houses, which one associates with certain districts in England
and France . . . The whole feeling of the entrance front of the house should be
one to be gained through easy flowing lines, dark masses of foliage, considered
quite as much from the point of view of winter effect as summer space and
quietness . . . No so-called, ornamental planting should be attempted . . . the
forms and textures should be all that is needed to give the feeling of dignity
and simplicity which the lines of the building themselves demand.*

*While in no way should the planting on R street look as though it were
intended to close out people's view of the place, it should in effect do this, but
by giving them interesting and pretty plants to look at, with the occasional
calculated glimpses of the place . . .*

*It is . . . suggested that the planting of this south front of the house be as in
a sense as permanent, and, if one may so say, impersonal, as possible, leaving
the more delicate arrangements to serve as attractive objects for the walks and
paths which will some day be worked out on the north slopes . . .*

Farrand then suggests possible treatments for the front of the house and for
masking the service road entrance. She continues around to the back (north)
vista:

*No definite suggestion is made with regard to the planting under the north
gallery as it is felt that this is one of the most important pieces of the planting
to be done, requiring both delicacy and solidity of treatment and where exactly
the right material should be used to get a continuous effect without coarseness
or monotony . . .*

The difficult problem of the North Vista would not be solved satisfactorily
until the 1950s. After many false starts, Mildred Bliss finally found a resolution
working with the engineer Robert Patterson and the architect Ruth Havey.

*On the northeast corner of the house two magnificent oak trees enclosed by the
low brick wall inevitably suggest the making of a green garden which would in
a sense be a part of the rooms looking out on it . . .*

It was characteristic of Beatrix Farrand to choose not a piece of sculpture but an important plant as the focus of her garden compositions. This Green Garden terrace, built around the two oaks, served as an outdoor room for large parties, the subdued palette of green lawn, ivy, southern magnolia, and hollies the perfect sober foil for women's colorful evening dresses.

The north side of the Orangery will naturally be flagged as it will be a pleasant place to sit on hot sunny mornings . . .

A semi-enclosure was made on the north side of the house. Called the Star, it was designed as an informal place for taking breakfast and tea. The floor was paved in a circular pattern, with lead figures of constellations. A marble fountain and basin, the Aquarius Fountain, and marble seats were set into the three-foot-high brick walls in the 1930s. Farrand writes:

The east front of the house really presents the hardest problem . . . The various suggestions as for shortening up the terraces in different directions . . . can hardly be more crystalized until studied immediately on the plan . . . it seems clear that the rose garden must be practically flat in appearance and that a large stone wall on its west side, if properly designed, would make a considerable part of its charm . . .

The first problem Farrand tackled was the terracing to the east of the house. As a general rule she maintained the natural contours of the land wherever possible, and she did so in many instances at The Oaks, where no terrace is without its pitch and no planting completely symmetrical. What makes the Rose Garden terrace so distinct is the contrast: it is the largest and flattest of the many terraces, and it seems all the more so in juxtaposition to the massive stone retaining wall that forms the imposing west border of the garden. This terrace, discussed by Bliss and Farrand at their very first meeting, was to become the Blisses' favorite part of the garden.

The lower herbaceous garden should, in the writer's mind, be a very much less prim design than the rose garden, with considerable masses of perennials, none of them large in size, but giving a sort of general friendly mixture of color and form and entirely different in type from the upper level . . .

East of the Rose Garden, down a double flight of stairs, is the Fountain Terrace. The two pools originally sported simple fountain jets at their center, their curbing copied from Edith Wharton's garden at Pavillon Colombe in France. "It is important that their curbs be allowed to become as mossy as possible," Farrand later instructed, "the fountains should appear to have been 'found' there and to be a part of the old plan." The terrace's "friendly" and "less prim" appearance was enhanced by vigorous climbing vines that cloud the terrace walls: trumpet vine, native porcelain berry, English ivy, autumn-flowering clematis. Farrand continues:

The pool below the herbaceous garden, with its grassy seats and slopes, may be made an unusual frame for an out-of-doors picture. It is so entirely romantic in type that all sorts of plants of the weeping-willowish will be appropriate . . .

Beyond the Fountain Terrace to the east, the Lovers Lane Pool, with its miniature amphitheater of brick-framed grassy seats (adapted from an open-air theater in Rome), is perhaps the loveliest area of the garden. The reflective pool with its delicate border of shiny, small-leafed plants—bamboo, weeping willow, and periwinkle—is transformed into a shimmering otherworldly glade each spring with washes of naturalized scilla, snowdrops, and daffodils. At the other end of the pool, opposite the amphitheater, Mélisande's Allée begins. In reference to the woodland section to the north, Farrand writes:

The contours and expressions of the ground will control the plantations more strongly than any other feature. The brook certainly could be widened ... and used as a mirror in which to reflect large plantations of azaleas and iris, or overhanging dark masses of hemlock, with water-loving plants growing on the still surface, and walks arranged on the different levels so that the plantings could be seen from above as well as from their own level. It is hoped that one ravine could be given over to a mass of azaleas, another to a plantation of Magnolias and crabs, and that a walk be arranged of the different varieties of lilac following the east boundary and in general making an old-fashioned "circular walk" which was so usually a part of every eighteenth century design. It is also hoped that a part of the grounds could be developed as a "Wilderness" where hollies, yews, ivies and spring flowering Magnolias and winter flowering shrubs would make an attractive walk to be followed in winter. Another part of the grounds should have a primrose garden, possibly surrounded by a nut walk. A large mass of 10 forsythia planted on one of the hillsides and in combination with blue Lungwort and daffodils will be attractive at its own moment, and in the writer's mind the development of the north part of the place should be on the lines of a series of interesting plantations, each thought out for a certain season, and easily reached by a good walk and yet not conspicuously in view when it is not at its best.

"The onrush of spring at Dumbarton Oaks fairly leaves one breathless before the great billowing mass of forsythia tumbling down two hillsides turned to gold," Mildred Bliss wrote of Forsythia Hill—a minimal, monochromatic ocean in the northwest section of the property, considered by many one of the glories of the garden. Lanning Roper remarked that "The late Lord Aberconway [owner of the magnificent Bodnant Garden in Wales] told me on several occasions that he considered [the forsythia] one of the finest bits of planting in America." Others have an opposite reaction. Some find the forsythia overwhelming, verging on vulgarity. Inarguably bright, the display lasts just two weeks.

Wildflower drifts along the Branch (the creek that runs north of Forsythia Hill) and plantations of mountain laurel, dogwood, and rhododendrons were planted within the twenty-seven-acre section of the garden that was not given to Harvard but turned over to the National Park Service in 1940. Never maintained well, the area gradually became completely overgrown. Restoration on the park began in 1992 by a local band of volunteers under the auspices of the Garden Conservancy. Beatrix Farrand continues in her letter of July 5:

The best place for the big kitchen garden is in the area between the present gardener's house and the east terrace ... The cutting garden should be thought out as a part of this scheme and espaliered and cordon, small fruit and large, should be planted on either side of the walks and also on the hillsides sloping down from the terraces to the garden. This would seem to tie the whole scheme of house, terrace and green garden, swimming pool and kitchen garden, into a unit ...

The Cutting Garden, with its pair of ogee-domed tool pavilions, still produces its rows of flowers each and every summer, but the proposed scheme for fruit tree espaliers, revisited in the early 1960s, was never fully realized. A small orchard stands on the hillside between the formal terraces and the lower levels. In recent years the new trees have been selected of ornamental rather than fruit-bearing varieties. With her encyclopedic letter Farrand sent preliminary planting lists both for the R Street plantation border and for a selection of more tender potted plants for the Orangery.

The topographical survey of 1922 reveals the land's dramatic physiognomy and what already existed on site—cow paths, roads, and remnants of the old

Above:
Beatrix Jones Farrand, c. 1925.

farm. In addition to the main house, barns, outbuildings, and a system of service roads are indicated. By and large, all remnants of the farm buildings and service roads were removed after 1922, much to the consternation of the garden staff, who ever since have had to hand carry in all of the plant material and machinery—including heavy lawn mowers. Astor Moore remembers that the garden staff resorted to using a series of logs "like the Egyptians" to help roll large trees to the interior areas of the garden.

Some rudimentary terracing had been in place before 1920, particularly to the east of the house where the drop of the land is quite steep. A cow pond and path are drawn in exactly the spot of the eventual Lovers Lane Pool and Mélisande's Allée. But in addition to what was already on site, the survey reveals how far Mildred Bliss had gone with the initial layout of the grounds as of July 1922. The swimming pool and tennis court, mentioned in her letter of July 13, were clearly in position. An orchard of apple, cherry, and peach trees had already been planted on the hillside between the house and the future site of the Kitchen Garden.

Bliss reacted with warmth and gratitude to Farrand's report. Happy to have found so compatible a collaborator, she wrote:

Your letter and its enclosure have made me purr with contentment. You have got it exactly, in every respect . . . We are very appreciative . . . and greatly touched that you feel as you say you do about the Oaks . . . When you return [from France] you will find the pool, loggia, tennis-court and orangerie almost finished. The means of exit from the two East windows of the living-room to the walled garden is still a puzzle, but after more reflection I am convinced that it is a garden, and not an architectural problem . . .

Beatrix Farrand's Landscape Practice

When Beatrix Farrand first met with Mildred Bliss in January 1921 at The Oaks, she was nearing fifty. Professionally, she was entering the most productive period of her career and the years in which she would create her finest gardens. It was also to be the most satisfying period of her personal life; eight years earlier, she had married the constitutional historian Max Farrand. Max, then chairman of the history department at Yale University and a noted authority on Benjamin Franklin, proved to be a good match. Beatrix introduced her husband to the pleasures of gardening, which he embraced with a passion, and he, in turn, taught her to enjoy both golf and fly-fishing. Yet her professional life remained extremely demanding. In October 1922, following Farrand's visit with Edith Wharton in France, the author wrote to Max Farrand complaining of the strain her niece was under:

I don't like the idea of Trix being so tired . . . but, as she says, it was no doubt the excessive efforts made to clear the way for departure that told on her afterward, for she seems a slave to her work in a way that ought to belong only to the beginnings—But I know how hard, how impossible it is to give advice about how other people—& especially people at a distance—ought to utilize a given fund of energy & ability . . .

Between the office and summer home in Maine, primary office in New York City (she kept both offices going at the same time), new home with Max in New Haven, and far-flung design projects, Farrand was always on the go. Although the family of Farrand's father (Edith Wharton's brother), Frederick Rhinelander Jones, was a wealthy one, her parents' divorce in 1896 had left Beatrix and her mother, Minnie Cadwallader Jones, in reduced circumstances. Wharton's *Age of Innocence* details the dramatic social costs of divorce for women of that generation. Beatrix still had some inherited income but now had to work ceaselessly to keep her mother and herself in something approximating their former style.

Minnie, Beatrix's ebullient mother, managed to keep up an active social presence. Sunday afternoons she opened her house to friends; artist John La Farge, sculptor Augustus Saint-Gaudens, and society portraitist John Singer Sargent were among the regular guests. Mrs. Winthrop "Daisy" Chandler described the scene in her 1934 memoir, *Roman Spring:* "[Minnie's] house . . . full of books and old engravings, was a refuge . . . Henry James was one of her intimates; he stayed with her all the time he was in New York."

Like Mildred Bliss, Edith Wharton, and Elisina Tyler, Minnie Jones worked tirelessly for war relief charities during World War I. She also suffered the occasional physical breakdown. Annually Jones traveled to Europe: to France to see Wharton, to Scotland to visit a cousin, and to England to see Henry James. She became her sister-in-law Wharton's literary agent in America. Wrote the author in 1918, "Minnie and Trix make up to me for my own wretched family, and all my thoughts and interests are with them."

Beatrix Farrand's landscape practice was no small enterprise, according to landscape architect and historian Diana Balmori, who interviewed Ruth Havey, one of Farrand's employees, in the late 1970s. Farrand's professional fees in the 1920s were equal to those of leaders in the field, and Havey found her employer "always very much in control." When Farrand traveled, she had a system where one or more of her assistants would board the train with her in New York; they would work together in one of the cars until their task was completed. The assistants would leave the train at the next stop, wherever it was, and return directly to New York. "Obviously," commented Balmori, "Farrand knew the problems of trying to run a small office and the pressures it put on one's time. She was a Type A personality; Havey told me that Farrand was very focused and very organized, and that they both shared an indefatigable need to obsess until they got things right." A similar description would be perfectly appropriate for Mildred Bliss.

Robert Patterson, a landscape engineer from Mount Desert, Maine, assisted Farrand in her work in later years and eventually assumed her place on the Dumbarton Oaks Garden Advisory Committee. He described the extent of her professionalism:

Her authority was so complete that she not only hired all the gardeners, but handled through her office all the payroll and all other costs of maintenance. She worked with phenomenal energy and thoroughness . . . A perfection of detail . . . characterized her work, and it often became blurred and lost without her critical eye and tireless hand. Even in her most formal designs, plants were paramount . . . It is commonplace to say that a garden is a living painting; it is not at all common to see one that has the quality of a good painting. Beatrix Farrand gardens did have that quality.

Farrand well understood the hardships of landscape architecture as a profession for women. She enumerated the difficulties in two lectures on the subject given about 1916:

Landscape architecture or gardening is usually supposed to be an ideal profession for women by those who know little about it except the general notion that women have pretty taste in colors and are fond of flowers. It is a profession that no woman should attempt who is not above, rather than below, the average physical strength and endurance . . . It sometimes means eight hours or more office work, making plans, drawing up specifications, and draughting . . . The work is physically hard, the hours long and traveling incessant, and steady nerves and a good temper are quite as important for a landscape gardener as a sense of color or design.

She listed as requirements for the profession:

1. Income enough to keep her alive without the practice of her profession as the money return is not large.
2. A strong body, resistant to bad weather and long office hours.
3. A good temper, common sense and the power to see the other's point of view, whether Nature's or the client's.
4. The desire to be a landscape gardener more than anything else in the world.

A Spirit of Collaboration

By early September Beatrix Farrand wrote to Mildred Bliss concerning the terracing and the Rose Garden. For each problem, she presented Bliss with several possible design solutions, along with accompanying illustrations. This method of decision making, this back-and-forth discussion and development of ideas, would remain the modus operandi throughout the project. She wrote:

Won't you please take these designs and see what you think of them.
If you would like a part of one adapted to another it can be easily done.
The whole thing is fluid and I want your help in arranging it . . . Do tear
up the designs as much as you will—mark them up and return them to
me with your comments . . .
Yours ever affectionately, Beatrix Farrand
P.S. The sample stone sent by Harris for the paving was too awful for words.
I have telegraphed him to that effect.

Spring

Previous pages:
Keystone in the arch to the Arcade;
single-flowered Japanese cherries in
bloom on Cherry Hill; Forsythia Dell;
saucer magnolias by the Ellipse.

Opposite:
Cherry and magnolia blossoms.

Below:
Detail of Magnolia conspicua.

Above:
View north from the Arbor Terrace.

Opposite:
The walk on Cherry Hill.

Above:
Wild violets mixed with crab apple petals.

Opposite:
View south through the Plum Walk,
installed in 1956.

Following pages:
The hillside along Mélisande's Allée.

Above:
Spring bulbs along Mélisande's Allée.

Opposite:
Blue scilla in the grass along Mélisande's
Allée.

Top:
Scilla flowers and winter aconites foliage.

Above:
Lily of the valley.

Opposite:
Terraced seats of the Lovers Lane Pool,
designed in 1923 and completed by 1930,
planted with blue scilla.

Following pages:
Tulips, crown imperial fritillaria, and
Johnny-jump-ups in the Herbaceous Border.

Top:
Spring planting in the Herbaceous Border.

Above:
Detail of the iron grillework off the
Rose Garden terrace.

Opposite:
The Fountain Terrace.

Following pages:
Wisteria draping the Arbor Terrace arbor,
designed by Beatrix Farrand and based on
a drawing by Jacques Androuet Du Cerceau.

Below:
View from the Rose Garden east to the
Fountain Terrace.

Bottom:
Lead mask of a river god purchased by
the Blisses in Paris in 1927 set into
the Fountain Arch panel, designed by
Beatrix Farrand in 1931, on the
Arbor Terrace.

Opposite:
View north from the Rose Garden.

Top:
Kidney seat designed by Beatrix Farrand.

Above:
Two seats and an urn sculpture on
Forsythia Dell, based on drawings by
Armand Albert Rateau.

Opposite:
Hedges of white azalea in the Star Garden,
installed in 1923.

Following pages:
View from the North Vista toward the south
facade of the house.

Chapter Three: 1922–1932

In December 1920, one month before Beatrix Farrand's initial meeting with Mildred Bliss, Lawrence G. White of the Manhattan architectural firm McKim, Mead and White visited The Oaks. White, the son of architect Stanford White, was married to Laura, Mildred Bliss's friend Daisy Chandler's daughter. White's firm specialized in the creation of palatial homes for America's wealthy and had also designed such new landmarks as Pennsylvania Station and the Brooklyn Museum. White's tasks at The Oaks would be all new construction. Already being discussed was a cluster of service buildings with a stable to be built to the west of the house.

Written documentation of work on the garden in those early years is scarce. However, within the archives at Dumbarton Oaks, there exists a series of dated plans and design drawings that provides the best record of what was designed, and when. "Swimming Pool and Terrace Plant Section," one of the earliest plans, was drawn in May 1921. The drawing places the pool to the north of the house, where it was, in fact, built—on the site of the former farm's manure pit.

In 1922 William James Gray was brought on as superintendent. Dedicated, with a thoughtful, easygoing manner, he presided over the gardens until his untimely death in 1937. Early on, Robert Bliss wrote to Mildred that "Gray is a treasure and Trix and Russell [Robert Bliss's private secretary] sing and chant his praises."

Gray was among a wave of trained estate gardeners who came to the United States from Britain at around the turn of the century. These gardeners' traditional apprenticeships on large English estates made possible the elaborate gardens of the Gilded Age. Gray was not only invaluable horticulturally speaking, he was a gentle "solvent" for the schemes of his two taskmasters: in his pleasant but authoritative way he translated their intentions into ideas that actually worked. By June 1922, the estate was fully functioning. More detailed plans for the swimming pool were drawn up that year as well as designs for the nearby loggia—a covered walkway with attached changing rooms and showers, which bordered the pool on the south side. A survey of the terrain and of the existing plants near the Orangery was also prepared as preliminary work on the terracing commenced.

Frederick Brooke had completed his renovations of the house within two years, finishing just about the time that Beatrix Farrand was beginning to shape the terraces in the east sector of the garden, where the ground was most steep. It was decided that the Rose Garden would be the largest of the new areas east of the Orangery, and that meant reconfiguring what terracing was already in place: sharpening it, dividing it into smaller and larger portions. The Rose Garden's construction would require the erection of a massive stone-and-brick retaining wall. Plans of November 1922 include details for the "Rose Garden Brick Pilasters" as well as an elegant bluestone paving pattern for the floor of the Lovers Lane Pool.

In the midst of all this activity, in January 1923 Robert Bliss was appointed United States minister to Sweden. Since his return to the United States, his foreign service duties had been for the most part ceremonial. He was the official United States representative during the stay of the Prince of Wales in San Diego, California, before being placed in charge of "ceremonials, protocol and related matters" for the Washington Conference on the Limitation of Armaments in Washington, D.C. (1921–22). Even when he had been based in Washington as chief of the Division of Western European Affairs, Robert Bliss's duties were of a formal nature, such as welcoming Georges Clemenceau, the former president of France—tame business after having lived through the Great War.

Left:
The Rose Garden during construction of the massive garden wall in 1922.

Below left:
The Rose Garden planted with boxwood slips, c. 1923.

Bottom left:
Woman and a Unicorn *at the back approach to Dumbarton Oaks.*

The Blisses, who referred to themselves as "professional nomads," were pleased with Robert's first full ambassadorship and with the opportunity to once more live abroad. And Sweden was not that far from Paris. As for The Oaks, Mildred had confidence that Beatrix Farrand and Lawrence White would keep the renovations going at a good clip although she would be in Stockholm for months or even years.

In 1923 White was brought in on a more official basis, "with a view to drawing up plans for the farm buildings." The "farm buildings" were a proposed new quadrangle arrangement to be located to the west of the house, which would contain The Oaks's "service group": garage, stable, machine shop, heating plant, greenhouse, and another small orangery, which later would become known as the Orchid House and which would contain a collection of orchids that Beatrix Farrand inherited from her mentor, Charles Sprague Sargent, following his death in 1927.

Plans, too, were under way to purchase additional property next door containing a charity, the Home for Incurables. White's engineering expertise would be needed when this structure was razed and the new property incorporated into the estate.

White also assisted Farrand as the engineer in charge of regrading the terraces, a delicate matter. Because the existing large trees were what gave the property its character, special care had to be taken that their roots not be disturbed by repositioning the soil. The trees had to be "honored," as Philip Johnson was to put it.

Farrand's massive first task was to generate the garden's fundamental plan. Her aunt Edith had written: "The inherent beauty of the garden lies in the grouping of its parts." It is in Beatrix Farrand's plan for the estate that her landscaping genius is most evident.

European Traditions Within an American Landscape

Michel Conan, director of garden studies at Dumbarton Oaks, believes that Farrand's greatest challenge was to unify the property: "When the Blisses bought The Oaks, it was not an exciting site, placed on the very top of a hill with 'little' views. The ground was very steep and was scarred by traces of the estate's former history." Farrand solved the problem, bringing it all together "fairly brilliantly," he believes, for he points out that her plan accomplished two different things: she allowed the place to speak for itself as an authentic American landscape, and then upon that landscape she superimposed a scheme that reflected the Blisses' belief that they were salvaging the best of European culture. Says Conan, "The garden is a statement of its time and of the then common assumption that the role of American artists was to develop from a continuation of European traditions." But beyond that, Conan sees in the plan a poetic rendering of the history of civilization in America:

In the original plan one could approach the garden, not from R Street, but from the back [through the park land to the north of Dumbarton Oaks], entering from the forest as if it were a "wilderness." And here Beatrix Farrand [in 1938] placed a statue of a young girl and a unicorn. In the Middle Ages the unicorn was a sacred animal representative of purity. It was so pure, in fact, that men could not approach it. The only way to catch a unicorn was to send out something equally pure—a naked virgin—into the deepest part of the forest.

It's like a fairy tale, and for the visitor who knew the story the statue was a symbol that they were in the wildest part of the forest. This use of symbols, this lightness, is a wink as if to say: You know we're playing a game, but isn't it fun.

The next segment of the plan is the walk from the forest to the stream at the bottom of the valley. Says Conan:

Here you see that the land is clearly inhabited. There are Robinsonian-like plantations of laurel and daffodils. There are a mill and a stone bridge made of rough-hewn stones, which in the iconography of the early twentieth century represented rustic America—the Arcadian history of the site. This picturesque scene in the valley is where Mildred Bliss rode her horse every day. It's like an illustration in a children's book.

That interpretation of an American landscape was just the first stage of Farrand's plan. Conan continues, "Superimposed upon this setting, up near the house, are features of European gardens—Italianate terraces and stairways, French *treillage*, Jekyllian borders—like the jewels of European culture: these are Mildred Bliss's contributions to the landscape." This two-part plan is Beatrix Farrand's expression of that contribution: a collection of jewels set into what already was there. "And of course," Conan adds, "this must have thrilled Mildred Bliss in a way that fueled further development of the garden."

As her plan evolved, Farrand oversaw countless large and small details. Garden enclosures, walks, and walls had to be staked out, and planting was required for major new trees and marker plants, such as the stately Irish yews that ground each end of the perennial border walk, which she and Bliss nicknamed "Mrs. Yew" and "Mr. Yew." The outdoor swimming pool and tennis court, already under construction, required new landscaping to blend them seamlessly with the rest of the property.

Farrand supervised the planting but freely called upon White for engineering and construction expertise—easy enough to do, since White's office was just around the corner from hers in New York. Farrand, in fact, made a practice of referring to herself professionally as a landscape gardener, as opposed to a landscape architect, stating that her realm was that of plants and soil—and leaving the built elements of any project to the architects and engineers and to her own drafters.

"The arts of architecture and landscape gardening are sisters, not antagonists," Farrand explained in 1897. "[Their work] should be done together from the beginning, one supplementing the other, but not, as too often happens, one crowding the other out."

Just as White was beginning his work on the service group, the Blisses decided that a new music room—a large space for receptions and musical performances—would be necessary. Once again, "honoring the trees" would be a major factor in siting this new room. Important surveys made in March 1923 included maps of the corner of R Street and Lovers Lane, where a natural cow pond was being transformed into the Lovers Lane (or Theater) Pool with a small grassy-seated amphitheater at the south end.

Sweden 1923

That spring, as the Blisses departed for Sweden, Farrand sent them her farewell:

Somehow there will be a rather drab feeling at the Oaks without you, & it is going to be very hard to find it empty on my next visit, & not be able to look

Top:
The rustic grotto on the south side of the Branch, now in Dumbarton Oaks Park, c. 1935.

Above:
The pergola in the valley along the Branch, now in Dumbarton Oaks Park, c. 1935.

Above:
Robert and Mildred Bliss during Robert's
tenure in Sweden.

forward to your little crow & laugh as you appear around a corner with the
faithful Mac [Mildred's dog] . . . I'm honestly glad for you & Robert that you
are going to an interesting post, within reach of France & Italy & away from
the fuss of local politics & the daily worries of the Oaks.

The Blisses saw Edith Wharton immediately upon their arrival in Paris, and
Wharton reported back to Farrand: "How delightfully & intelligently Mildred
& Robert Bliss spoke of your work & of the pleasure of having business
relating with anyone so full of understanding."

That fall the Blisses made a quick trip back to Washington, meeting with their
designers to work out the next steps in the property's development. But after
that visit, they were abroad to stay. Beatrix Farrand and Lawrence White
kept in touch with Mildred Bliss through a series of regular written reports.
At first, each designer wrote at least monthly.

In November 1923 Mildred Bliss wrote to Farrand from Paris: "Your two
beguiling letters of September 13th and October 14th have come and filled us
with delight as well as homesickness . . . We think the proposed scheme for
the box-garden on the knoll just right." The box garden was the area to the
east between the house and the Lovers Lane Pool, created with some of the
old Blount boxwood bushes. This scene was later described by Farrand in her
1941 *Plant Book for Dumbarton Oaks:*

On either side of the walk leading toward the Apple tree, queer old box bushes—
rather grotesque and out of shape—are purposely set irregularly on either side
of the walk. This little area has been known as "Cocky-Locky's Garden," as the
fantastic shapes of the Box scraps look like overgrown topiary figures and give
an accent of the unexpected.

In her 1980 annotations to the volume, Diane Kostial McGuire noted that
Cocky-Locky's Garden had "changed from the desired grotesque to the
demure" due to regular pruning; more recently, an effort has been made to
restore the fantastic effect.

Mildred Bliss wrote to Farrand again from Paris two weeks later: "I had a
beautiful evening reading your wire . . . and looking at the blueprints [of the
Lovers Lane Pool] . . . [I] send you the enclosed diagram of Edith's most
delightful reflecting pool at St. Brice." The "Edith coping" Bliss went on to
suggest for the Lovers Lane Pool may have been the model for the coping
surrounding the two small pools in Dumbarton Oaks's Fountain Terrace.

Based on their talks of the previous fall, Lawrence White drew up the plans
for the service group quadrangle and in January 1924 mailed the blueprints
to Stockholm. Robert Bliss wrote to White: "Your letter of January 8th,
addressed to Mrs. Bliss, as well as the blueprints were received a few days
ago. She has not been well for some time [Mildred was a lifelong sufferer
from back pain and arthritis] and it is not possible to reply as yet . . . This
will, however, not prevent your making the specifications and getting
estimates . . ."

For her part, Farrand was busy developing the landscaping for the new
quadrangle, as well as completing the grading scheme for the Lovers Lane
Pool—a complicated design, since the pool sits at the base of one of the
steepest sections of the property fifty feet below the floor of the Orangery.
Following a bad rainstorm floes of mud would occasionally wash down
the hillside and collect at the base of the Lovers Lane Pool retaining wall,
requiring the gardening staff to haul the soil out in wheelbarrows.
This situation was recently remedied by replanting the hillside in liriope.

Prices were determined for the casting of one lead pineapple finial, for the fixtures, and for the glazed windows that would be used in the new greenhouse. Anthony DiLorenzo, a sculptor in New York, was hired to make the model for the finial for a price of forty dollars. Then, for one hundred dollars plus freight, one copy of the DiLorenzo pineapple model was cast of Hoyt Hardlead by United Lead on Broadway. The pineapple, a symbol of hospitality, appears several times in the decoration at Dumbarton Oaks.

In March Lawrence White mailed the finished blueprints for The Oaks's farm buildings to Stockholm. He was stunned by Robert Bliss's response in a letter dated April 19:

My dear White,
I am sorry that so much time has elapsed since the receipt of your letter of March 21st . . . but I have not found time until now to write you fully regarding the plans for the new buildings at "The Oaks." My wife and I have talked over this matter . . . with frequency and care and we have reached the conclusion that it is superfluous to have a stable at "The Oaks" . . . I am sorry to come with this eleventh hour suggestion of change . . . but I am sure . . . we are eliminating a source of needless trouble, worry and expense. With cordial remembrances in which my wife would join were she not in Paris, believe me,
Very sincerely yours,
Robert Woods Bliss

White, perplexed, immediately sought Farrand's advice: "Have you any idea as to the rearrangement? I am in despair; the drawings and specifications for the stable building were completely finished, even down to fancy ventilation and stall fittings!" He impatiently wrote again eleven days later: "I am still waiting to hear." After one more week, Farrand responded. She would, she told White, write the Blisses and "put the question a little more sternly. I feel it will be a great mistake to destroy the quadrangle you have so admirably planned."

In fact, the quadrangle was not destroyed. As Robert Bliss had pointed out in his letter, repositioning the other new buildings required at The Oaks—specifically the gardener's and butler's cottages—would "preserve the appearances of the plan." The quadrangle construction, with the Blisses' modifications but without White's "fancy ventilation and stall fittings," went forward as scheduled. Thereafter Farrand saw to it that all details of the service group quadrangle were resolved on site.

The new greenhouse, a part of the service group, was of particular concern to Farrand; her letter to White concerning its specifications illustrates the degree of detail for which she now was responsible. Dated December 9, 1924, the letter covers eight different points encompassing the division of the greenhouse compartments, the suggestion of a cellar for cut flowers under the potting room, recommendations of specific temperatures to be maintained, earthen (not concrete) walkways and brick floors, the ventilation system, bids, and other specifications.

In December 1924 White was tackling the difficult problem of siting the new music room. Spring found Farrand still resolving details of the Lovers Lane Pool while making initial plans for the Green Garden—the area immediately to the north, or back, of the house. She also designed the Kitchen Garden arbor, a simple, traditional structure over which two leads of a single grapevine would in time grow.

Correspondence from Mildred Bliss to White dated March 5, 1925, confirms the high priority given to existing plantings in siting considerations:

As you say, the place for the proposed music-room is obviously where the orangerie now stands. We have known this all along, but nothing would induce us to part with that Ficus Ripens. As for the beech-tree, we could not face [losing] that either, so all things considered, if there is to be a big room, it still seems to us that it would have to be north of the east wing . . .

Would you also please have a try at this idea: Scrap the loggia, the platform in front of it and the swimming-pool and see if a building could be put up there, running east and west with a flat roof on a level with the green garden, thus continuing that terrace of grass and Vinca . . . Is this possible or am I quite mad?

Mildred Bliss's "mad" idea was taken seriously enough that a wood frame was set in place and photographed to illustrate its effect. "I enclose two of my lamentable drawings to show better than does perhaps the above text just what my notion of the change is," she adds. (The Blisses not only wrote to White and Farrand with their suggestions, they frequently sent along sketches and photographs to convey a certain idea or detail that they wished their designers to try.)

Four months later, Robert Bliss was again visiting The Oaks and reported on the progress to his wife:

Its just too hard to bear having to come back here without you when the whole place breaths your unfailing taste and your delicate appreciation of beauty . . . If only you were here this minute—! Trix is wild to have you come back—and does not cease to bemoan your absence . . .

Trix and Larry came out . . . and we went to service group. This is working out better than I had expected and will be a real success . . . Everything is "coming along" splendidly altho' the work that has been done is of such a nature that it does not show up except as one examines closely with knowledge of what existed before. The amphitheater pool is greatly improved and the vista down the allee between the maples too lovely. Gray's scheme for a walk with bricks is an excellent one, while the tennis court is a real success! Now what do you think I did about 7 o'clock? I took a swim in the pool! It was delicious.

Gray's scheme for a walk down the allee between the maples—a narrow brick ribbon following the winding cow path through what was to become Mélisande's Allée—has been called one of the first examples of an earthwork by garden conservationist Giorgio Galletti, a 1999 fellow at Dumbarton Oaks and the director of the Boboli Gardens in Florence: "The path, called Mélisande's Allée, is not wide enough for two: it is simply the *line* of the path—a ribbon—to delineate the form of the landscape." Farrand's own comments bear out Galletti's contention:

It is . . . necessary to keep this walk narrow in order not to dwarf the scale of the width of the allee and the height of the trees . . . The position of the walk was decided after many stakings, much thought, and many changes, and its width was reluctantly determined upon when it was seen that a four or five-foot walk changed the whole scale of the allee so that it was a tree-bordered walk, rather than an arch of trees under which a narrow path winds its way.

The Early Years of Beatrix Farrand

For all their similar interests and shared passion for Dumbarton Oaks, Mildred Bliss and Beatrix Farrand were of very different characters and temperaments. Bliss was a petite, red-haired beauty: worldly, imperious, fun

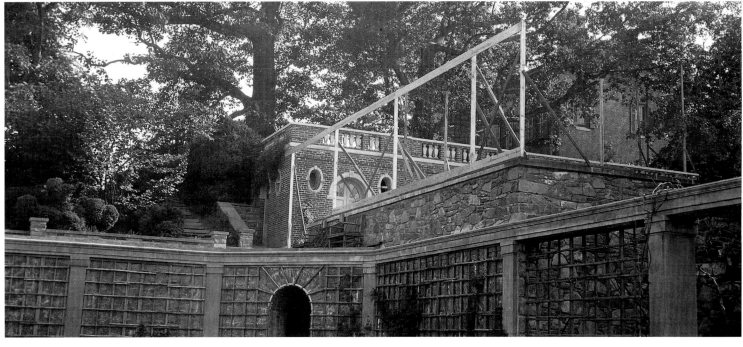

Above:
Mélisande's Allée being staked, with a new row of silver maples (at left) planted by the Blisses.

Right:
Mélisande's Allée in spring.

to be with. Farrand had lived much of her life in the shadows of her vivacious mother and her famous aunt, Edith Wharton. People who met Farrand have described her general manner as cold. But according to Robert Patterson, "I suppose 'aloof' is a fair description of her outward manner, but she was far from aloof to people who interested her. She was simply ruthless in weeding out those who did not." According to Farrand's biographer, Jane Brown, she may have suffered a number of nervous collapses, including one in 1920 just before commencing her work at The Oaks.

Beatrix Farrand's own background allowed her to understand what her clients needed to know and to shield from them what they did not. It is not surprising that she took on ever more of an intermediary role between the Blisses and White as work on The Oaks progressed.

Farrand was the primary landscape architect to work at Dumbarton Oaks: she spent eighteen years on the preliminary planning and planting of the gardens (nine while the Blisses were living abroad), and she would go on to advise Mildred Bliss on garden matters and on the purchase of rare books and prints for the Dumbarton Oaks Garden Library Collection for an additional eighteen years, until her death in 1958.

A product of the pre-professional era, Beatrix Farrand was largely self-educated with regard to her landscape training. Ruth Havey, by contrast, thirty years younger than Beatrix, was schooled in the modern mold: she was a 1920 graduate of Smith College, with degrees in both landscaping (1923) and architecture (1934) from the Cambridge School.

The overall design of the gardens was developed by Farrand very early on, as was the next step, the landscaping plan. The following stage, the architectural features at The Oaks, was developed, in large part, from a set of drawings prepared in 1929—shortly after Havey was hired by Farrand—by the French artist Albert Armand Rateau. Havey's main influence can be seen in the fourth phase of the garden's design, the finishing elements of hardscaping and furnishings; her major contributions came after about 1936. In the late 1950s and early 1960s, Havey worked with Mildred Bliss to redesign several sections of the garden. Although few of her designs were implemented, the Italianate Pebble Pool is a glorious exception.

Farrand once explained that her love of gardening was a family trait going back "five generations." As a young girl, she helped her parents lay out the roads and planting beds at the family's then new summer home on Mount Desert. Contrary to fashion, Farrand's mother, Minnie Cadwallader Jones, preserved the native flora wherever possible, while most neighbors typically removed all native growth, replacing it with huge lawns and exotic specimen trees. Farrand would attribute her lifelong love of native plants to her mother's early example.

Early on Farrand had considered becoming a professional singer, but in 1890 she met Mrs. Charles Sprague Sargent, a botanical illustrator and sister-in-law of the artist John Singer Sargent—a frequent visitor to Minnie Jones's Sunday salon. The illustrator was the wife of Professor Charles Sprague Sargent, the first director of Harvard's Arnold Arboretum. The Sargent brothers had been born and raised in Europe by "culture-seeking" American parents.

When Mrs. Sargent learned of the young woman's interest in landscape, she invited Beatrix Jones, then twenty years old, to stay with the family and study informally with her husband at the arboretum. At that time there were no formal schools of landscape architecture: the way to enter the profession

Above:
Emily Drayton Taylor, ivory miniature of
Beatrix Jones as Diana, c. 1895.

was to apprentice in a professional landscaping office, something not suitable to a young woman of Beatrix's social position. And so, in 1892, wrote Beatrix, she became both "the grateful guest of Mrs. Sargent and the hard working pupil of Prof. Sargent at the arboretum." She would work with Charles Sargent for periods of several months over the next few years. That, as well as a course or two on drafting, was the extent of her "professional" training.

But Charles Sargent's words took, and fifty years later, Farrand reiterated some of his principles in a garden-club lecture. First, she said, "Make the plan fit the ground and do not twist the ground to fit a plan"—in other words, take cues from the natural character of the site, keeping the design appropriate to its location. Sargent also advised, Farrand said, "Study the tastes of the owner," so that each scheme expressed the vision of the client, not of the designer. These instructions were responsible for two distinctive characteristics of Farrand's work: first, her work always blended seamlessly into the natural landscape; second, each project was unique, each garden, to some extent, reflecting the client's personality.

Sargent had more advice that Beatrix heeded. He instructed, "Look at great landscape paintings . . . travel widely in Europe and see all the gardens you can; learn from all the great arts for all art is akin." Twice Beatrix set off to Europe for six-month tours of the gardens of Italy, France, Germany, Spain, and Great Britain. The study gave her work an authority, a sureness of proportion, that less-traveled American landscape designers could not match.

Beatrix Jones was twenty-three years old at the time of her first trip and twenty-seven for her second, in 1899. She kept a diary of her impressions. These brief notes indicate what she considered significant: suitability of design, correct proportions, fine details of ornament, good use of specific plants, and the clever manipulation of light and shadow. On her first trip to Europe, an important stop was Italy:

Saturday, March 30th, The train to Frascati: *Villa Conti . . . The fountain at the end of the main axis of the villa is very effective . . . the ilexes [not a holly but a tree similar to the American live oak] are superb on this terrace and the ground was blue with periwinkles . . . [the] fourth terrace, which was evidently once a bosque [small woodland] with walks in squares, [had] a large fountain in the middle, being the center of the design . . .*

Rome: *. . . gardens of the Vatican . . . the loggias were once covered with brightly-colored mosaics and the ceiling frescoed with such mixed subjects as the creation of man and Leda and the swan. The whole effect . . . so light and airy and such perfect taste. The gates also which led into the elliptical courtyard are beautiful, and they also were lined with mosaics . . . This garden having been altered and tinkered with by so many different people cannot be criticized as can those of a single designer. It is not a whole, it is a collection of gardens put together inside a wall . . .*

Tuesday, April 2nd, Io Viterbo: *In fact the grounds seemed the best combination I had seen of the landscape and the architectural styles. The transition was almost imperceptible, and from a formal fountain one walked into a deep wood and then out on a grassy lawn with a tennis court on it. The place had an air of refinement about it, and one felt, more and more . . . that the ghosts of the people who lived here must come back . . .*

Villa Alforza Casanini: *curious place . . . The grounds have a charm although they are not very good and being entirely of one key, and therefore rather monotonous, of course it is hard to make a garden of the steep side of a crater . . .*

Villa Gambaria: . . . *the only beauty of the formal Italian garden lies in its perspectives, effects of space which really do need space, the proportions of the parts to each other and the works of art in the shape of fountains and statues which emphasize the design.*

Boboli: . . . *is one of the most-refined. This air of distinction is, I think, given it by the great use of good statues. There are no ludicrous figures like those at Caserla, these having all the charm and grace of the Renaissance.*

In 1895, while in England, she had the opportunity to meet a variety of garden designers and architects through introductions from Charles Sprague Sargent and other family connections. She visited with the Arts and Crafts–style gardener and writer Gertrude Jekyll (yet to publish her influential book on the use of color in the garden) and with William Robinson, the leading exponent of the new naturalist school of gardening. She saw the gardens of the architect Harold Peto, a close friend of Henry James who was in the forefront of the classically inspired school of landscape design. Decades later, at Dumbarton Oaks, influences can be found in Farrand's work from each of these designers.

Borders, for instance, were planted in the subtle graded hues favored by Gertrude Jekyll, whose original ideas on color theory were being formulated just at the time of Farrand's visits. William Robinson's call for more natural designs is reflected in the exuberant plantings of narcissus, wildflowers, and native trees in the wilder areas of the garden and along Mélisande's Allée. Harold Peto's careful use of large, architectural structures in gardens is most apparent in the elegant arbor that Farrand constructed along the west wall of the Herb Garden (now the Arbor Terrace).

Her second European garden tour coincided with the first official meeting of the American Society of Landscape Architects. Because Beatrix Farrand had, by this time, done a significant amount of professional work and was known to several of the group's organizers, she was elected one of only eleven charter members of that organization, even though she was unable to attend.

Drawings and Mock-Ups

Beatrix Farrand and Lawrence White were suddenly working double time: the Blisses would be in Washington in a matter of months. A May 1926 visit was scheduled. Robert Bliss wrote to White: "Needless to say we are keenly looking forward to our return to The Oaks . . . You will recall that [Mildred] has not seen the place since it was occupied by the Home for Incurables [September 1923]."

After three long years of design by mail, how thrilled Mildred Bliss must have been with what she saw. The garden plan was now set. To the east the terracing was complete—including Mildred's favorite room, the Rose Garden, where the slim slips of boxwood already had begun to frame the geometric patterns of rose beds. The margins of the property, planted in 1922 with holly and box, lent a new feeling of privacy to the estate. The quiet Lovers Lane Pool and Mélisande's Allée, the Kitchen Garden, and the swimming pool with its Italianate loggia, if not all completed, were at least complete transformations of what had been there three years before.

Everywhere in the garden, Mildred Bliss would notice the care with which each element was rendered, from the patterns in the brickwork to the finishing of the arbor posts, all fashioned to the standards of craftsmanship

Above:
View of the arch ornamentation and lead book box on the Arbor Terrace, designed by Beatrix Farrand.

she was familiar with from Europe. And there was more. Designs at Dumbarton Oaks, British landscape architect Lanning Roper explained, had been decided upon from plans and literally hundreds of sketches passed back and forth between the two women by letter:

Details of materials and patterns for the laying of paving and the construction of walls, mock-ups of garden ornaments and wrought iron gates were endlessly set up and the process of trial and error carried on until the right solution was evolved . . . All decisions were made jointly by Mrs. Bliss and Mrs. Farrand.

The mock-ups were full-scale representations of garden elements made of painted plywood for items like walls or furniture. Patterns were drawn on large sheets of paper for details of wrought iron, and sculptural details were modeled in clay (and sometimes modified there on the spot) and set in place where they were to be installed—to try and create, as closely as possible, the effects that these additions would have in the garden.

This utilization of mock-ups is generally employed in most gardens where ornament, gates, etc. are being selected. Only in this way can one be sure as to scale, for all too often garden ornament which seems enormous when viewed in the showroom looks dwarfed when it is moved into its chosen position in the landscape . . . The same criteria were used for planting. Stakes were made to determine the optimum height of a hedge: the scale of huge boxwood trees on the formal terraces, and the point at which the pollarded pears and willows should ultimately be stopped so as not to block the view from the upper terraces.

Beatrix Farrand sometimes used trees in innovative fashion. The pollarded Kieffer pears are a good example. Planted at the wall beneath the herb garden, their trunks grow up above the terrace, creating framed "lookouts" of the view to the north. Farrand also used European espalier techniques, rarely seen in America. The southern magnolias planted alongside the house were rigorously clipped and trained to stand as neatly as vertical hedges.

Farrand's second challenge at The Oaks, Michel Conan believes, was to bring unity to Mildred Bliss's eclectic collection of enclosed gardens:

The garden has many similarities to Hidcote and to Sissinghurst: they are roughly contemporaneous and all three are collections of garden rooms. What makes Dumbarton Oaks something entirely of its own is the skill Beatrix Farrand had of leading one through the garden.

Beatrix organized the garden plan on a grid with three east-west axes and two north-south axes. It's a very strong plan and could be stiff and boring—formal in the bad sense of the word, but it's not.

For instance, if you look at some French baroque gardens, you look at them once and you immediately understand everything. At Dumbarton Oaks, Beatrix Farrand's plan gives you a strong sense of unity, but very cleverly, she does not reveal the plan in any obvious way. To the contrary, she plays with the crossing of the axes so you fail to see where they intersect—it's no coincidence that she was nicknamed "Trix."

Traditionally that crossing would have been just in front of the building. At Dumbarton Oaks, one pair of perpendicular axes meets in the air, over the descent to the Rose Garden; another meets *inside* the building. "You can't find the crosses," says Conan, "and that is all done in a playful sense. She is playing tricks with the visitor's memory: just when you think you're making sense of the plan, you discover that you've been fooled."

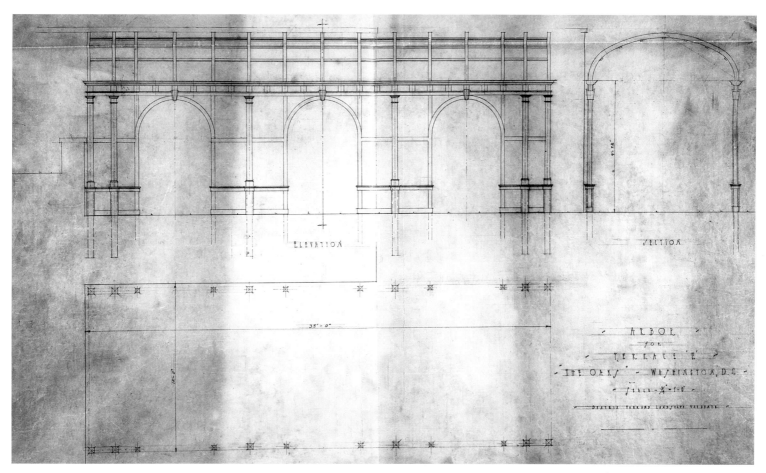

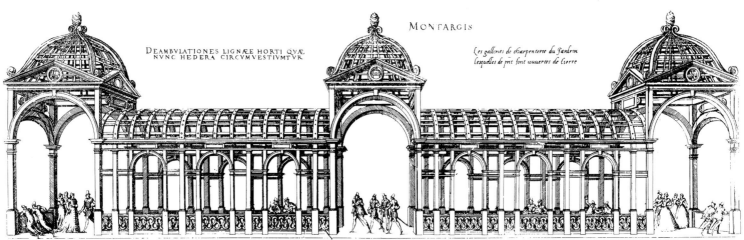

DEAMBVLATIONES LIGNÆE HORTI QVÆ
NVNC HEDERA CIRCVMVESTIVMTVR

MONTARGIS

Ces galleries de charpenterie du Iardin
lesquelles de prnt sont couuertes de lierre

Top:
Elevation of the Arbor Terrace arbor by
Beatrix Farrand.

Above:
Jacques Androuet Du Cerceau, design for
the arbor at Château Montargis,
sixteenth century.

Left:
Full-scale mock-up of the Rose Garden
bench, c. 1927.

Below left:
The Rose Garden bench.

Top:
Allyn Cox's mural in the loggia facing the swimming pool.

Above:
Re-creation of the loggia mural in mosaic, 1965.

The best views into several of the garden rooms are highly off-center, he adds—in the case of the Rose Garden, for example, looking to the southeast from an upper balcony lookout point. He comments, "Each view was planned to offer tantalizingly leading glimpses to what lies beyond. It takes only three or four steps to move from one enclosed garden into someplace totally different—and you instantly forget where you have been just moments before. As you walk through the garden, that sequence is repeated." In other words, the garden plan is about motion, "guiding one's steps in ways one does not even realize are happening."

White's service group quadrangle was almost completed. Foremost in everyone's mind was the knotty problem of where the music room should be positioned. A consensus was reached at the May meeting, but three months later the Blisses had another idea: siting the room at the northwest end of the house. They wrote their designers from aboard the S.S. *Leviathan:* "This new plan is much more to our liking than any of the previous ones, for it ties the music room closely to the house . . . we await with much interest your opinion after you have studied the plans." That new plan would prove to be the final one.

While in the United States the Blisses paid a visit to the artist Allyn Cox. The following year Cox was commissioned to create a mural at The Oaks on the classical theme of Diana and Actaeon; it was installed out-of-doors on the wall of the loggia facing the swimming pool. (The painting began to deteriorate almost immediately. In 1965, under Cox's supervision, it was reproduced rather crudely in mosaic.)

Farrand's design drawings from 1926 on continued to address refinements to the Green Garden, swimming pool, and loggia area—all areas that, until recently, had been possible sites for the music room. She also began to work on several new areas of the garden, including the Lilac Circle and areas along the creek to the north of the property, now outside of Dumbarton Oaks proper.

Further Developments in the Garden

Not everything Beatrix Farrand tried in The Oaks's gardens withstood the test of time, either due to physical conditions on site—too much shade, a soil disease—or due to a change in taste on the part of Mildred Bliss. The Lilac Circle was a case in point.

In Beatrix's 1941 *Plant Book* she notes that the lilacs planted in the Lilac Circle did not live long in their shady position and were soon replaced with *Philadelphus coronarius* and *grandiflorus*, fragrant mock orange. The mock orange was replaced in the 1940s with a later-blooming variety of lilac. However, under the direction of consulting landscape architect Alden Hopkins in the 1950s, these lilacs, prone to powdery mildew, were replaced with the newly fashionable camellia. Hopkins's camellias suffered from a deep freeze in the 1980s and were taken out. In the late 1990s new camellias were put back in.

Beatrix Farrand continued to take on other commissions. In 1923 Yale University was added to her growing roster of campus projects. In the autumn of 1927 she was asked by Mr. and Mrs. John D. Rockefeller Jr. to design a garden for their summer home at Seal Harbor on Mount Desert. Meanwhile in Stockholm, the Blisses had initiated a push for Edith Wharton to receive the Nobel Prize in literature. Although at the peak of her career, Wharton did not win the prize, which was awarded to the Italian writer Grazia Deledda and to the French philosopher Henri Bergson.

For the next three years, letters to Lawrence White in the Bliss file deal almost exclusively with matters relating to the Dumbarton Oaks house and music room. But in 1928 White mentioned that "Mrs. Farrand is working out a scheme for the steps from the green garden down to the loggia level [the Horseshoe Steps], which present a very difficult problem. I am sure, however, that she will solve it successfully, as she has in the seats and steps of the theater, which are simply delightful. The same is true of the amusement pavilions in the kitchen garden." These three elements—the theater seats and steps, the ogee-domed amusement pavilions in the Kitchen Garden, and the Horseshoe Steps—are among the most elegant constructions in the garden. Farrand wrote of the theater seats in her *Plant Book*:

These seats have been adapted from the well-known open-air theater on the slopes of the Janiculum Hill at the Accademia degli Arcadii Bosco Parrasio [a Roman garden designed in 1725 by Antonio Canerari]. The shape of the theater at Dumbarton was copied from the one in Rome, but the slopes surrounding the Dumbarton theater are far steeper than those of the Italian hillside and therefore the seats are considerably raised from one level to another. In order to give seclusion to the little theater, we have surrounded it with cast-stone columns, also baroque in design, and taken in their essential ideas from Italian gardens of the baroque period. The cast-stone columns are connected with a split natural-wood lattice in long horizontal rectangles. These trellises are covered by both deciduous and evergreen creepers, such as Honeysuckle, Ivy and Jasmine.

The garden historian Jane Brown cited a precedent for the two squat garden pavilions in the seventeenth-century gardens at Traquair House, near Peebles, in Scotland, but there are many examples of fancifully topped garden houses, including some similar designs in Swedish gardens, or at Mount Vernon, which just as likely could have served as inspiration.

"The whole place looks ravishingly lovely with everything bursting into bloom," Lawrence White wrote to Robert Bliss. Like his father, Stanford White, Lawrence took a great interest in his client's interior furnishings. In his letter he adds that he has found, through an antiques dealer, "a very good fountain," a photograph of which he had already forwarded to Farrand.

That fountain was just one of a number of treasures White had discovered. There was a sixteenth-century stone well from Rome; Verona marble columns at $450 each; "a fountain from the garden of Pope Pio IV ($1,500 price fob dock N.Y.)"; and an antique Spanish mantle of pink stone at $1,250—all items from Howard Studios, Inc.—Garden Ornaments, Mantels & Antiques, NYC. (White informed Mr. Howard: "I am keeping the photograph of the columns and the fountain, which may prove interesting, but I am returning herewith the fireplace which will not do.")

As early as 1924, White mentioned to Robert Bliss that he had asked the French designer Armand Albert Rateau, who was in Paris, to keep an eye out for garden ornaments for the Blisses. Mildred Bliss, too, was sending back jardiniere from Europe. Shipments from the late 1920s and 1930s included urns, statuary, and a dozen rose pink marble tables and benches from Paris—all of them to find new homes at The Oaks.

From Sweden to Buenos Aires

The Blisses managed another brief visit to Washington in May 1927. But first they stopped off in Paris. Amid Mildred's daily fittings at the House of Worth

Above:
One of fifteen Italianate cast-stone columns designed by Farrand to border the Lovers Lane Pool, backed by a screen planting of bamboo.

Right:
Amphitheater at the Lovers Lane
(or Theater) Pool, c. 1932, which was used
as the setting for several concerts.

Below:
Rustic stone bridge over the Branch,
now in Dumbarton Oaks Park.

Below right:
Pavilion in the Kitchen Garden with
ogee-domed roof covered in hand-made
Italian tiles.

Bottom:
Elevation and cornice detail of the Kitchen
Garden pavilions, now used as tool sheds.

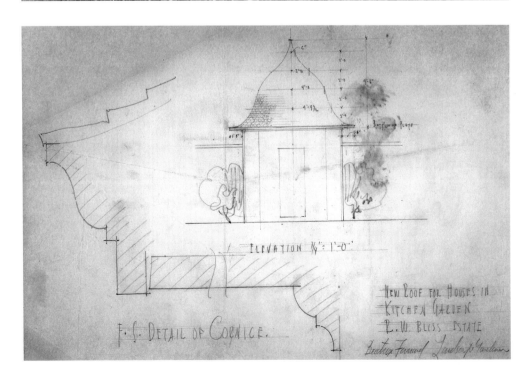

and frequent lunches with the Tylers and the Gays, she met the designer Armand Albert Rateau. Rateau was one of the least known yet most renowned of the French designers working in Paris in the 1920s and 1930s; his small but exceedingly wealthy clientele was too exclusive to gain him much public exposure. Rateau established his own design practice and workshop in Paris in 1920, after having served in the French army in World War I. His clients included the couturier Jeanne Lanvin (for whom he designed her famous black-and-gold perfume bottle), Cole Porter, and the French government, for which he refurnished ministry offices and various foreign embassies.

Rateau has been described as a "neoclassical modernist"; his style derived from an interest in Greek and Roman antiquity. His best-known designs were pieces of opulent furniture made of cast, polished, and patinated bronze, with cushions covered in ocelot. But Rateau's work covered a whole spectrum of styles, and he considered himself primarily a sculptor. In his workshops were built furniture and plasterwork of every period and style; his craftsmen even wove custom fabrics.

Mildred Bliss arranged for Rateau to create a distinctive wood ceiling and a floor for the new music room at The Oaks. One month later Lawrence White was in Paris to deliver the blueprints to Rateau. The high style of Rateau's environment can be imagined through a note written by White to Robert Bliss: "I spent the afternoon with [Rateau] and was absolutely fascinated . . . Did you see the platinum room he is making for the Cole Porters?"

At the same time at Dumbarton Oaks, the plan for a small stone bridge to cross the stream in the valley north of the house was developed, as well as elevations for the Lovers Lane Pool columns, stone caps for the R Street gate piers, and iron hinges for the large R Street gates. (The large wood gates, designed by Beatrix Farrand and installed in the brick walls facing the street sides of the property, were almost all replaced in the 1950s by Mildred Bliss and Ruth Havey with less private, wrought-iron designs. One of the original gates, very much in Farrand's Arts and Crafts style, is still in use on the 32nd Street front to the left of the entrance to the Study Center.)

In the midst of this activity, in 1927 Robert Bliss was posted as United States ambassador to Buenos Aires, Argentina. Also in 1927, Max Farrand was appointed as the first director of the Henry E. Huntington Art Gallery and Library, a study center, library, art gallery, and garden in Pasadena, California. The Blisses were returning to South America, while Beatrix Farrand would necessarily further divide her time, devoting several months each winter to her duties as the new director's wife.

Rateau

White informed the Blisses in February 1928 that "the house should be completed in about three weeks." In fact it took ten months longer as well as a personal appeal from Paris by Mildred Bliss—an event noted in her diary as "Rateau ATTACK." The ceiling's installation was marked by a gathering in Washington of almost the entire design team. Mildred Bliss, Rateau, White, the house's master carpenter, and others all met at The Oaks on December 14 and 15. Rateau's new "antique" ceiling was celebrated as an unqualified success.

Spurred on, as she had been the previous year by Farrand's work in the garden, Bliss quickly decided that Rateau should undertake another project.

Below:
An early mock-up for the Horseshoe Steps, which was discarded before 1930.

Bottom:
Armand Albert Rateau's drawing number eight, showing a figurative sculpture that suggested the scallop form for the fountain in the Horseshoe Steps.

She asked him to turn his attention from the interior of the house to the outside. White's office quickly prepared measured drawings for several areas of the garden where something of a more architectural nature was needed: gates, piers, fountains, seats. Rateau, in turn, produced some thirty-two design drawings, keyed to White's scale renderings.

Rateau's 1929 drawings were to guide many of the architectural features built in the garden over the next forty years; as Dumbarton Oaks archivist James Carder has shown in his unpublished catalog, many of the designs done after that date, formerly attributed solely to Beatrix Farrand, were directly derived from these thirty-two drawings. In a sense, the trio of Farrand as landscape gardener, White as architect/engineer, and Rateau as artist was not unlike the team much favored by Farrand's most beloved predecessor, André Le Nôtre.

In 1998, while working in a basement storage area, Carder came across an envelope containing reproductions of thirty-two unsigned drawings. Previously he had come across puzzling archival photographs of mock-ups in place in the garden that were labeled on the back "Rateau dummies." Carder pursued the connection: "I knew that [at Dumbarton Oaks] Rateau had been the designer/maker of the music room ceiling and floor, the oval room, and the founders' room paneling. As a design student I was familiar with Rateau's work on interiors, but I had never read that he had worked much in gardens," or, he adds, that Rateau had worked at all in the gardens at Dumbarton Oaks.

Of the newly discovered designs, he says, "Rateau was the source of two types of design . . . pedestal sculptures, to be peppered through the property as focal points; and complicated figurative groupings, or centerpieces, that look very baroque, or at best rococo, in feel." Whereas several of the more conservative pedestal sculptures were incorporated at The Oaks, "None of [the figurative groupings] were used in the Bliss/Farrand design period."

The graceful shell fountain in the Horseshoe Steps leading from atop the loggia down to the swimming pool is a good example of how one of Rateau's ideas was modified by Farrand and Bliss. In the Rateau rendering, the shell fountain was originally a freestanding monument, but as realized it was incorporated into the undulating oval of the Horseshoe Steps.

Carder asks, "Did neither Beatrix Farrand nor Mildred Bliss like what Rateau did?" He adds, "With Mildred Bliss you always have to add, or was it simply too expensive to do?" Carder speculates that Farrand, the more conservative of the two women, might have been particularly opposed to what she considered Rateau's excesses. In addition to Rateau's drawings, Carder also discovered a typed list in the archives that he believes to have been Farrand's. The numbered list of comments corresponds with Rateau's thirty-two drawings. The notes range from "perfect" to "to be suppressed" to the most common entry, a smug "fine, if done here."

In general, Farrand preferred the simple Arts and Crafts style or, in larger estates such as The Oaks, Arts and Crafts mixed with a restrained neoclassicism. Furthermore, the United States had just entered the Depression; Rateau's flamboyance was not appropriate. As a result of the economic crisis, Farrand had suddenly lost a good deal of her campus work and was receiving few new commissions. Clearly she felt some need to retain control at The Oaks. "It's very likely that Rateau was paid a fee for his efforts, but was not otherwise engaged to stick around and carry out production," says Carder. "Farrand was thinking that without Rateau around she would be able to get his designs *right*, according to Mildred Bliss's and her own taste."

Opposite top:
Rateau drawing number thirty-one, showing a shell atop a column for the Horseshoe Steps.

Top left:
Mock-up of Rateau's column-and-shell fountain.

Top right:
The fountain for the Horseshoe Steps, a modified version of Rateau's design.

Opposite center:
Drawing of the front-door steps at Dumbarton Oaks, probably prepared by Lawrence White for Rateau and labeled in French and English.

Center:
Beatrix Farrand's design for urns for the front-door steps, presented as a mock-up for Mildred Bliss's review.

Opposite bottom:
Rateau drawing number two, showing a pineapple finial and gate post for an opening in the Rose Garden wall.

Bottom left:
A mock-up of Rateau's pineapple finial, used to determine the correct proportions.

Bottom center:
Farrand's reworking of Rateau's finial as installed at the gate to the Rose Garden.

Bottom right:
Drawing of Farrand's urn design for the front-door steps.

Right:
Full-scale rendering of the wrought-iron gate for the Rose Garden.

Far right:
The Rose Garden gate, c. 1932.

Below right:
Gate surrounding the Gardeners Cottage (now the temporary home of the Dumbarton Oaks archives).

Bottom right:
Farrand's 1928 design for the Gardeners Cottage gate.

Opposite top left:
Rateau drawing number twenty-four for the west end of the loggia on the south border of the swimming pool, showing a covered walk ending with a vase atop a low wall.

Opposite top center:
Farrand's design for the loggia vase, installed after 1930.

Opposite top right:
Farrand's drawing for the pedestal and base, a modification of Rateau's design, c. 1930.

Opposite center:
The Bowling Green trellis, c. 1933.

Opposite bottom:
Farrand's design for the French-style treillage for the Bowling Green.

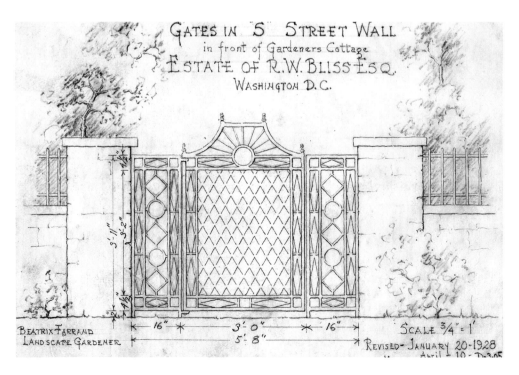

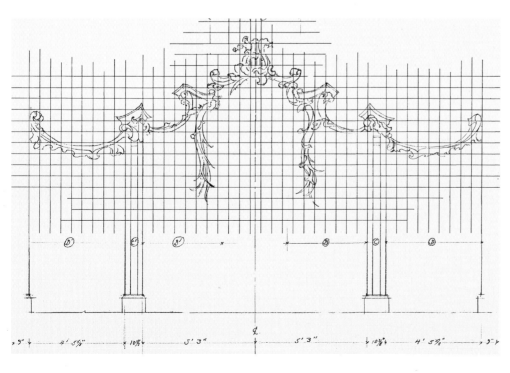

Right:
The swimming pool with weeping cherry trees, standards, and potted plants, c. 1935.

Below right:
The west end of the swimming pool before the application of the rocaille finish.

Bottom right:
An early Farrand design for the west end of the swimming pool.

More practically, there was also a question of copyright. Rateau, who was very clear in his contract as to the artist's commission, died in 1938. Before 1938 Bliss may rightly have been cautious about making use of Rateau's designs. But even as early as 1929, the insertion of a little of Rateau's style—an inimitable dose of French chic—was enough to place the Blisses' garden on a par with those of her friends in Europe.

Features and Ornaments

Mildred Bliss wrote to Lawrence White in December 1929: "Your letter of November 21st . . . with the account of the tapestries [for the music room], as well as the photographs, has put us quite aquiver with excitement . . . It is quite clear that without you and Mrs. Farrand we should not be living in Argentina—a somewhat anomalous blessing, perhaps . . ."

Drawings at The Oaks in 1928 and 1929 concentrate on hardscape elements: gates, stone bumpers to line the driveway, flowerpots, lattice panels for the interior Orangery roof, coping for the fountain north of the music room (in what was formerly the Copse), the paving pattern for the potting shed floor, and so forth. The west end of the swimming pool (based on Rateau sketch number twenty-three) was a major undertaking, as were the planting plan for the Herbaceous Border and a design for cold frames to line the south side of the new service area greenhouse.

Drawings from 1930 include a pedestal for the terra-cotta vase near the loggia (Rateau's drawing number twenty-four)—another prime illustration of how Rateau's design, specific to the site, was modified and adapted by Bliss and Farrand. Other drawings include details of the tassels-and-rosette ornament for fencing in the Bowling Green. Farrand designed a delicate French-style wooden trellis, crowned with a lyre, for this garden in 1931.

The west end wall facing the swimming pool had been a particularly difficult problem to resolve. Archival photographs illustrate exactly how Farrand proceeded and with what detail. Rateau's design for the Bowling Green pool was clearly a source of several of the salient elements: the grotto-like rocaille-finished back wall, the vases, the fountain.

The final designs, in every case, were the result of much trial and error; every decision was debated back and forth between Farrand and Bliss. Almost thirty years later, Mildred Bliss described the method by which the women worked:

Never in all the years did [Farrand] impose a detail of which she was "sure" but which the owners did not "see"; and never were the owners so persuasive as to insist on a design which [Farrand's] inner eye could not accept.
A deepening friendship born of intellectual challenges, of differing tastes and of the generous tact of her rich wisdom made the years of close association a singularly happy and most nourishing one.

In 1933 Robert Bliss retired from the United States foreign service. Thirteen years after purchasing the property, the Blisses were finally ready to come back to The Oaks to live.

Summer

QUOD SEVERIS METES

Previous pages:
Wheat sheaf in Pebble Pool;
Pebble Pool with the Bliss motto and
signature wheat sheaf, designed by Ruth
Havey in 1961; Rose Garden with beds
bordered by bluestone and obelisks on wall
similar to designs illustrated in Gertrude
Jekyll's Garden Ornament.

Top:
Azalea covering the wall at the west end of
the loggia.

Above:
The wall at the west end of the loggia with
snow-dusted plants.

Opposite:
Winter jasmine overhanging the wall at the
west end of the loggia and at the base of the
Horseshoe Steps.

Top:
View of the Horseshoe Steps from above.

Above:
The west end of the swimming pool.

Opposite:
The Horseshoe Steps.

Following pages:
The walk leading to the Lovers Lane Pool
with the Terrior Column, installed in 1934.

Above:
Planter on the wall of the Fountain Terrace.

Opposite:
View of the Terrior Column and
surrounding daylilies from the gate to
the Fountain Terrace.

Following pages:
The Cutting Garden.

Top:
The west end of the Herbaceous Border with
a teak and iron bench designed by Beatrix
Farrand before 1935.

Above:
"Mrs. Yew," one of the two Irish yews at
either end of the Herbaceous Border.

Opposite:
View from the Cutting Garden south over
the Herbaceous Border and the orchard to
the Arbor Terrace.

Following pages:
Oak and aluminum bench under the Kearny
Baldacchino, with a lead hood designed by
Farrand in 1932, on the Fountain Terrace,
with the Quod Severis Metes bench in the
Rose Garden directly overhead; the Ellipse.

Above:
Antique Provençal fountain in the Ellipse
planted with canna and water lilies.

Above right:
The hornbeam colonnade, planted by Alden
Hopkins in 1958, surrounding the Ellipse.

Right:
Carved-stone Provençal fountain in the
Ellipse.

Top:
The Urn Terrace between the Beech Terrace and the Rose Garden.

Above:
Pebble cornucopia designed by Ruth Havey in 1960 as a test for the stone mosaic in the Pebble Pool.

Opposite:
The urn for the Urn Terrace, carved by Frederick Coles and based on a terra-cotta original purchased by Robert and Mildred Bliss in Paris in 1929.

Following pages:
Path from the gatehouse inside the R Street wall, running next to a katsura tree and Japanese maple on the East Lawn.

Top:
Interior of the Orangery with potted plants
intended for the Arbor Terrace.

Above:
Creeping fig in pendant forms covering the
Orangery walls.

Opposite:
View of a magnolia through the doors to the
Orangery.

Following pages:
Path leading to the Lovers Lane Pool.

Chapter Four: 1933–1937

In 1933 the view looking southeast across the lawn from the front door at The Oaks—atop the undulating plateau at the highest point in Georgetown—had changed very little since 1801, when the house was built and the land still used for farming. By the time the Blisses retired to Washington, what had changed was some careful landscaping along the margins of that lawn—a staggered planting of trees and evergreen shrubs (all plants chosen for their small, glossy, evergreen foliage)—that effectively make a protective veil between house and street.

The drama lay behind the house, to the north. Beatrix Farrand wrote of the area: "Paved and enclosed spaces [the Beech Terrace, the Green Garden, the Star Garden, and the North Court] were made for constant outdoor use, as the owners felt the gardens were an integral part of the design and they used the spaces opening from the drawing room and music room as a part of the rooms they adjoined." Monochromatic in planting—entirely green—but varied in texture, these gardens, strung along behind the house, provide panoramic views of the rest of the gardens, which fan down the slope from the plateau to the parkland beyond.

The gardener Donald Smith, who came to work at The Oaks just after World War II, recollects that in his earliest days there arborists were brought in every few years to trim the tops of the silver maples that formed Mélisande's Allée in order to extend the view from the Green Garden and Beech Terrace belvederes out beyond the estate across Rock Creek Park to where the Connecticut Avenue bridge at the entrance to Kalorama was visible.

While the Blisses were in Argentina, a few years earlier, Mildred Bliss had begun arrangements for two surprises to mark the occasion of their return to The Oaks. She had written to White, as early as 1930, about a surprise for Robert, for "what goes in the music room over the mantle." Mildred's plan was to have a bird's-eye painting of the estate created in the manner of Renaissance lunettes by Guisto Utens. In the mid-1500s, Utens painted similar views of the Medici estates in and around Florence for the *sala grande* of the Villa Ferdinande. Ernest Clegg, a military illustrator, was selected to create Robert's map, which would be based on an aerial photograph. That map was Mildred's first surprise.

Above:
Ernest Clegg, watercolor map of
Dumbarton Oaks, 1933.

Clegg's large watercolor of the estate still hangs over the fireplace in the music room, where it was installed in 1935. Although now faded, the painting is the clearest image of how the gardens looked in the early 1930s, when the Blisses were in residence. It is on that map that, for the first time, "Dumbarton Oaks"—a combination of the property's land-grant title and its last given name—appears as the name of the estate.

Testimonio Amicitiae

Mildred Bliss's second surprise was for Farrand—a monumental thank you from the Blisses in the form of a tribute inscribed on a large limestone plaque, to be installed permanently in the balcony of the Green Garden. Although Bliss began planning this surprise in 1930 in Argentina, it was not completed until 1935.

The first party logged in the Blisses' Dinner Party Record was a luncheon on June 18, 1933. Delphiniums bedecked the table, roast squab was the entree, and Beatrix Farrand was the guest of honor. At that luncheon, in addition to formally expressing their gratitude to Farrand for all of her good work at Dumbarton Oaks, Mildred and Robert unveiled their plan for the Green Garden plaque.

Top:
Tribute panel to Beatrix Farrand in the
wall of the Green Garden.

Above:
Robert and Mildred Bliss standing in the
Herbaceous Border, c. 1936.

Disarmed by the gesture, Farrand wrote of it to Edith Wharton, who shot back: "Your letter from Georgetown, just received, is such a joy that I must answer it at once. What a perfectly delightful 'geste' of Robert & Mildred's, and how it warms my heart to think that you have such devoted & appreciative friends." Ruth Havey designed the plaque and lettering. The Latin inscription translates to:

May kindly stars guard the dreams born beneath the spreading branches of Dumbarton Oaks.
Dedicated to the friendship of Beatrix Farrand and succeeding generations of seekers after truth by Mildred and Robert Woods Bliss

Many years later Mildred Bliss explained the convoluted story of that "geste":

When we were living in Argentina we wanted to pay a tribute to Mrs. Farrand in some permanent form, and an inscription placed in the Green Garden, which all of us love so well, seemed the appropriate symbol of our friendship. So one day I thought, and the [inscription] came to me . . . This expression expressed our thoughts, but, being in English, lacked privacy. So we decided to translate them into Greek . . . Next we tried Latin . . .

It was Professor Hendrickson at Yale who opened our eyes to the dual mode of the distich and the dedication and who finally interpreted our original intention in the smooth and serene rhythm that you see cut into the stone.

The definitive inscription, as Bliss hinted, was difficult to achieve; there is a file of more than fifty letters, written over a period of a year, in which different translations by various scholars were tried. Bliss worked directly for the first time with Ruth Havey, Farrand's drafter, on this secret project.

Mildred Bliss's life continued to whir along at a pace that was quite unlike "retirement." Summer in Washington, with its numbing mix of high temperatures and high humidity, is rarely comfortable. She wrote to a friend:

Since our return . . . we have hardly had one hour alone or free from the unexpected. Washington seems to be a through-fare for the whole world and . . . [they] usually have a reason, either to talk politics or collections (for we see a good deal of museum people). Or social reform, or because they are going South or coming North, or are sailing for some other land and want letters of introduction, or because they want help for a protegee, or wish to inveigle me into committee work, etc. . . . and although I don't lead a social life by day, seldom going outside our own gates save to a concert, I find we keep in fairly close touch with the essential currents.

Beyond Dumbarton Oaks

The aftershocks of the Depression were causing the Blisses to rethink their new situation. Mildred wrote:

There has been much death and many sadnesses and financial collapses among our circle of friends, and the management of the Casa Dorinda, and my sense of imminent change and consequent desire to finish the work before the storm breaks, has kept us in a ferment of concentrated effort and decisions . . . The beauty of the garden, the pleasure and healthfulness of the swimming pool, have been a constant delight, but, even so, it has been an effort to think clearly, and the tempo has, of necessity, been very reduced . . .

The Depression also had negative effects on Farrand's career, significantly reducing her supply of new and ongoing projects. Nevertheless, critically speaking, she was at the high point of her career. In July 1934, four hundred members of the Garden Club of America met in Bar Harbor—Farrand's home turf—for three days. The opportunity to visit her work on the island, including Reef Point and the Eyrie, was undoubtedly a highlight of the event.

In 1932 Farrand received an important commission, a project that would be perhaps, second only to Dumbarton Oaks. A former client, Dorothy Straight, had married and moved to Devon, England. There she and her new husband, Lord Elmhurst, were busy converting an old manor, Dartington Hall, into a liberal, progressive school. In 1932 Farrand was asked to help advise them on the fifty-five-acre estate, where she was to work for the next four years. But first she suggested that Dorothy Elmhurst take a look at Dumbarton Oaks the next fall, while she was in the United States. Dorothy did visit The Oaks, and wrote to thank Mildred Bliss for the opportunity:

It is a revelation of course to see what you have done, and when Mr. Gray showed me a photograph of a bare hillside and explained that this was the site of the present garden, I understood something of yours and Beatrix's genius. What endless variety there is in that garden, and each step of the way seemed to open out into an entirely new experience. I think I have never seen such a lovely pool as the one that lies deep in the shade with the ivy covered amphitheater behind it. That particular spot seemed to me more beautiful than anything I had ever seen in Italy or anywhere else, and then again my heart leaped when we reached the ellipse.

The box Ellipse, so dominant on the Clegg map, no longer exists. The design consisted of a ring of large boxwood bushes surrounding a low, ivy-rimmed pool sprouting a single jet of water. Such monochromatic schemes were typical rooms of respite in Edwardian gardens. Wrote Farrand in her *Plant Book:*

The Box Ellipse is one of the quietest and most peaceful parts of the garden . . . At one time planting was made under the big Box making the wall surrounding the ellipse, but it was found that the simpler the whole unit was kept, the more effective it was, and the more spacious and quiet its design.

The hedge, by 1935 seriously overgrown, was completely removed by 1958. Several schemes to redesign the Ellipse were tried, including one in 1958 by landscape architect Alden Hopkins that featured lead masks. It was again reworked in the early 1960s, following Farrand's suggestion of "an open colonnade on the north, through which could be seen the far hillside of Clifton." That design, with hornbeam trunks forming the colonnade and an antique stone fountain at the center, still stands.

Top:
Beatrix Farrand in France, 1934,
while visiting Edith Wharton.

Above:
The Box Ellipse, 1934.

Edith Wharton

It was not until 1935 that the finished limestone plaque with the tribute to Beatrix Farrand was installed. To mark the occasion, Mildred Bliss sent Edith Wharton a new set of photographs of the garden as well as a copy of the inscription itself. With genuine astonishment Wharton wrote to Farrand: "The photographs from Dumbarton Oaks and the beautiful inscription came . . . and I didn't wonder that your legs were cut from under you when you saw that lovely thing and read those beautiful words."

Farrand's design drawings from 1934 include the "Mr. Yew Seat." That seat, at one end of the Herbaceous Border, was later replaced by a low stone retaining wall. A marble bench for the North Vista, a "classic chair" for the

Above:
Aerial photograph of Dumbarton Oaks,
c. 1965.

Opposite:
Rudolph Ruzicka, map of the garden, 1935.

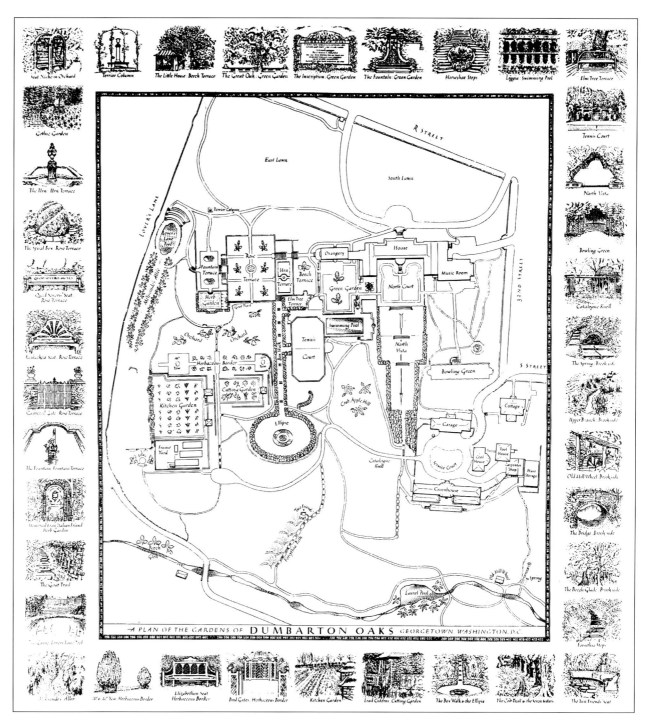

Top:
Mildred and Robert Bliss at home
at Dumbarton Oaks.

Above:
Max and Beatrix Farrand at home at
Reef Point.

Green Garden terrace, and the delicate Aquarius Fountain for the Star were also drawn that year.

Farrand wrote that the Star was "a place designed for more-or-less intimate outdoor groups of friends. The Chaucer quotation 'O thou maker of the whele that bereth the sterres and tornest the hevene with a ravisshing sweigh' surrounds the paved circle, and set in the corners of the stone frame are lead figures of certain of the constellations: Aries, Capricorn, Pegasus, and the Phoenix . . . Almost all the planting surrounding the Star are of white Rhododendron mucronatum (Azalea indica alba)." Bliss clearly had retained her interest in astrology. The stars, to her, were a part of the natural world, and the constellations a part of the cultural history that she sought to celebrate at Dumbarton Oaks.

In 1935 Mildred Bliss was fifty-six years old and Beatrix Farrand sixty-three. Farrand brought Edith Wharton up to date on personal matters:

I stopped to see Mildred at Santa Barbara . . . You will have seen telegrams telling of her mother's death. It is very touching to me to see how deeply attached Mildred was to her mother . . .

Mildred's attachment to Dumbarton Oaks is really almost like an attachment to her own child, and her pleasure was in consequence great when she knew you had liked the album of the "Oaks" pictures which she had sent you. She has deep in her heart the hope that you may come over to this country as she wants to show you her work.

It has been desperately hard for [Mildred] to carry on without the good sense and balance of Robert, who has been Aztec-ruining in Central America . . .

Shortly after this letter was written, Minnie Cadwallader Jones, Farrand's mother, died unexpectedly from pneumonia. That fall, perhaps at Max's instigation, the Farrands made the decision to turn Reef Point, where Minnie had first laid out the grounds in 1883, into a "little horticultural institution," with display gardens, a library and meeting room, a publications program, and potentially, visiting scholars. In fact Reef Point was to become something of a mini–Dumbarton Oaks, wholly horticulturally oriented, which prominently featured the native flora of Maine. Beatrix Farrand was to immerse herself in this project for the next twenty years.

Worn and weary with the strain of her mother's death, Mildred Bliss set sail for Europe with Robert on the *Golden Arrow* in December 1935. Christmas was spent in Paris with the Tylers. Edith Wharton reported to her niece in April that "Mildred looked very thin, but was bursting with activity . . . I have had a letter from Rome, where she seems to be seeing everybody and enjoying everything. What vitality . . ."

In addition to gossip and news, horticultural cross-pollination went on among Edith Wharton and her circle of friends. Farrand wrote to Wharton in 1936 with the latest news of some of her horticultural trials on the West Coast: "Our little Madeiran gardener in California writes me excitedly that some of the new South African bulbs are already up and abloom and . . . I am twittering to get out to see them . . . If the Lachenalias bloom out of doors in California, I shall twit you with them and ask if you want any." Wharton, in reference to Farrand's comment on South African bulbs, wrote, "So here is a final p.s. to say that Lawrence Johnston [the creator of Hidcote] grows the Afrikunders successfully, but with the most-complicated soil mixtures, and I doubt if I could do that."

Farrand had added in her letter to Wharton that Bliss had "started on a winter campaign of entertaining, concerts, queens and, best of all, Kenneth Clarks who are, I believe, for the moment at Dumbarton Oaks." Sir Kenneth Clark, the British art historian, had already become a part of Wharton's circle. They first met when he lived at Villa I Tatti, where he studied with Bernard Berenson. As he later wrote, "But when I met her again *The Gothic Revival* had been published, and Edith (it is one of the greatest compliments I have ever been paid) saw in me a fellow craftsman; and we became friends . . ."

Clark described their visits: "The first night I would tell her of all the extraordinary human situations that had developed since we last met, and she would giggle like a girl." He added, "Novelists live on material of this kind."

New Influences

With Max Farrand at the Huntington and Mildred Bliss now the owner of the Casa Dorinda, both the Blisses and the Farrands were spending a considerable part of each year in California. Mildred and Beatrix quite naturally became involved in a horticultural project on the West Coast: the Santa Barbara Botanical Garden's Blakesley Garden.

Back on the East Coast, Beatrix Farrand's 1937 designs for Dumbarton Oaks include an elegant little drawing of the bench for the balcony in the Herb (later Pot) Terrace. This spot was to become one of Mildred Bliss's favorite places. Into her eighties, she would come down to the balcony at about five o'clock every afternoon, just after the grounds had been closed to the public. She would sit and pause and gaze out over her garden, past Rock Creek Park, all the way to the distant Connecticut Avenue bridge.

In January 1937 Farrand, Bliss, and a young woman named Anne Sweeney began work on the Catalog House, the first public educational feature planned for Dumbarton Oaks, where visitors could stop and look up information about the plants they observed in the garden. In February Farrand informed Bliss: "The catalog house has been wickedly long delayed in its carrying out because it takes an absurd amount of time to verify and review the different names [of plant species]."

Farrand was still sending Bliss monthly project reports. In May she asked: "Have you done any 'dummying' and is there progress on the lilac circle trellis and some of the various experiments you meant to try for the north side of the herb garden, the forsythia vase, etc.?" Bliss and Ruth Havey had continued working on new designs for the garden, including fanciful chairs for the Star Garden based on Orion and other astrological figures. Clearly Bliss was in the mood for something new.

James Carder observed that in the 1920s and 1930s Bliss visited with the Walter Gays at Le Breau and with Edith Wharton at Sainte-Bryce and saw their elegant French-style décor: "And suddenly all that Anglo-American mahogany that [the Blisses] had in Washington, and which was listed in their 1926 inventory—the Queen Anne this, the Chippendale that—was gone!" Carder continued, "By 1937 it is Louis XV this and Louis XVI that—painted and dainty and very French. I think Mrs. Bliss simply decided that she liked that style better. And she looked at their gardens and decided that she wanted a little more French flair at Dumbarton Oaks, too."

Mildred Bliss *had* changed and would continue to do so; Beatrix Farrand, on the other hand, always held fast to the turn-of-the-century Arts and Crafts style. Wood gates for the Herbaceous Border, with delicate carved

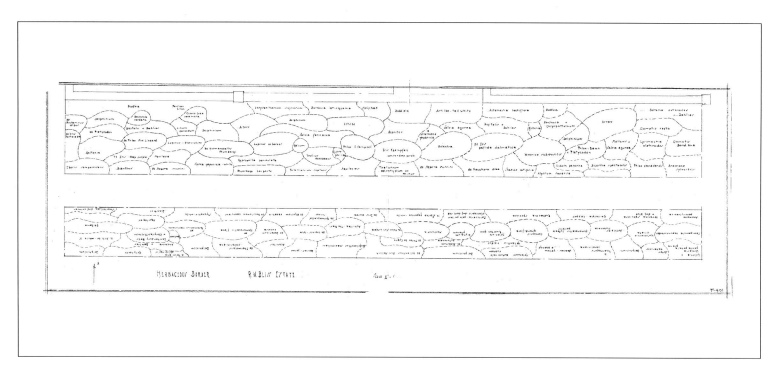

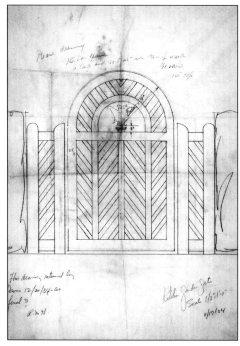

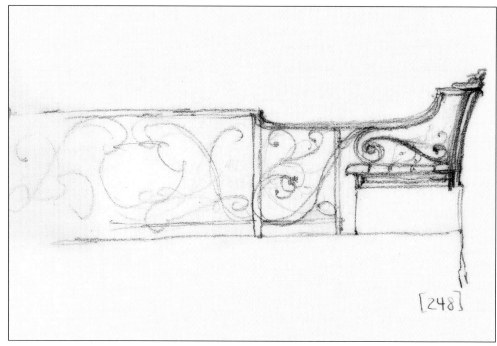

Top:
Beatrix Farrand's planting plan for the Herbaceous Border.

Above:
An early rendering of the gates for the Herbaceous Border, with a bat in the central arch.

Above right:
Ruth Havey's preliminary sketch for the balcony on the Herb (later Pot) Terrace.

Right:
Farrand's gates for the Herbaceous Border, installed in 1935.

wood thrushes alighting atop the gate posts, were designed by Farrand and installed at this time.

The Precision of Art

Beatrix Farrand had just landed in Canada following a visit to France when she received word of her aunt's death on August 11, 1937. Edith Wharton, "that machine of perfect precision," as Farrand once described her, weakened by three bouts of flu and a stroke, had died peacefully in her sleep. Wharton had been cared for during the last difficult period of her life by Elisina Tyler. She left her library to her godson, Colin, the son of Kenneth and Jane Clark.

In the late 1960s, Kenneth Clark wrote a BBC television series on the history of art. He gave voice to the aesthetic philosophy of Bliss, Berenson, and Wharton:

Across [the Pont des Arts in Paris] for the last one hundred and fifty years, students from the art schools of Paris have hurried to the Louvre to study the works of art that it contains, and then back to their studios to talk and dream of doing something worthy of the great tradition. And on this bridge how many pilgrims from America, from Henry James downwards, have felt themselves to be at the very center of civilisation? . . .

Ruskin said: "Great nations write their autobiographies in three manuscripts, the book of their deeds, the book of their words, and the book of their art. Not one of those books can be understood unless we read the two others, but of the three the only trustworthy one is the last."

Clark, in essence, had put into words what the Blisses were working to create for American scholars at Dumbarton Oaks—the full experience of Western civilization—through books, music, artifacts, and gardens.

Sometime in the midst of the turmoil of Wharton's death, Beatrix Farrand asked to see the latest designs that Bliss and Ruth Havey had been working on. Several items, however, provoked outright outrage, such as "New Swing for Terrior": "You may imagine how my eyes popped out of my head when this typical merry-go-round seat appeared. You will have to help me as to the reason for having one seat face away from the view you had so delicately achieved by the placing of the roof . . ."

Within days Bliss wired a reply: "So glad to have sour [*sic*] letter which will receive detailed answer next week on departure house full guests . . . from devoted = Milrob." With the passage of a few weeks, Farrand, cooled, responded: "The main business in the long professional letter [of August 28, 1937] has already been attended to by letters to Davis and Miss. Havey . . ."

Farrand regained her equilibrium following Edith Wharton's death, but the loss took a toll on everyone. Mildred Bliss wrote to Daisy Chandler, who had been Wharton's frequent traveling companion:

You have been more than usually in our thoughts since the twelfth day of August when cables and telegrams and a telephone conversation with Max Farrand brought us news of Edith's death . . . To Elisina and Royall [Tyler], it is a heavy blow . . . There is much yearning over my dear Beatrix and my lost Edith, the stimulus of nearly forty years . . .

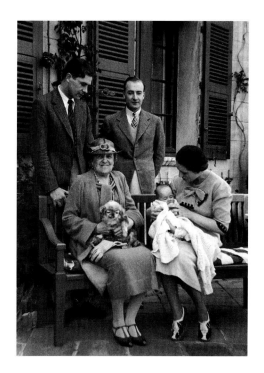

Top:
Edith Wharton and the Tyler family, Hyères, France, April 1935.

Above:
Ruth Havey's drawing for "New Swing for Terrior."

149

Chapter Five: 1938–1947

"For ten days I've been hearing that Mr. and Mrs. Bliss were deeding the estate or its collections—or both—to the William Hayes Fogg Art Museum of Harvard University," reported Jean Eliot in the January 16, 1938, edition of the *Washington Herald*. "Mr. Bliss says: 'There's nothing to it' . . . But the tale won't die down."

No sooner had the Blisses returned to Washington, Robert Bliss was to explain, than the "constantly increasing visits of students and scholars" began. They came to examine the artifacts in the Byzantine and pre-Columbian collections and to make use of the nearly sixteen-thousand-book library at Dumbarton Oaks. Clearly, it was more than they were prepared to handle.

The Blisses had other concerns. There were rumors of another war in Europe and thus the thought that Robert might be called back into service at the state department. Of more immediate worry was Robert himself, who had been suddenly taken ill while the couple was in Montecito. They had gone to California to close the Casa Dorinda following Anna Bliss's death. Robert's illness resulted in the Blisses staying in California far longer than expected. Recuperating, Robert was forced to remain in California for much of the next four years. Despite this, work in the Dumbarton Oaks garden went on at a brisk clip.

Farrand sent Bliss a report of her fall 1937 tour of the estate, including a list of the seven most important design projects immediately before them: "Finalities," a plaque to be set into the Rose Garden wall where, eventually, Mildred's and Robert's ashes would be interred; designs for the "Green garden lanterns"; the design for planting along the music room wall; a lamp for the garage; the Forsythia Arch, a large arched portal to mark the footpath from the valley along the creek up Forsythia Hill; the "Front Door tablets," three large panels with inscriptions about the site and its history that were to be set into the wall at the proposed entrance to the future Study Center; and "millions of other things."

Increasingly weary, in her next letter to Bliss Farrand comments, "I realize it is a nuisance to have a half-speed engine running alongside two express engines like you and Robert." But even for Mildred, the constant round of visitors, concerts, charity work, scholars, and entertainments became trying. In 1938 she was approaching sixty. Despite the considerable inheritance from her mother, Bliss now was responsible for managing two large estates—Dumbarton Oaks and the Casa Dorinda ("a serious white elephant," confided Mildred to a friend)—and their costs were huge.

Necessary economies were being put into effect at Dumbarton Oaks. "Gray has already cut seven men from his payroll, of which one is a greenhouse man," Farrand reported to Bliss. "He says the cut is absolutely 'to the bone' and that no further reduction can be made." The total garden staff now numbered thirty. A small nursery near the Quarters Building had also been established to propagate some of the shrubbery and perennial plant needs. Such an on-site nursery was in keeping with English estate gardening traditions, as well as with Farrand's own penchant for self-sufficiency.

Upon completion of her fall survey of the garden, Farrand told Bliss, who was still in California, "I hope you will see the blue Nymphaes [water lilies] at the West end of the Swimming Pool, as they were entrancing in their flower; also the group of Fuchsias on the North side of the Loggia, where it seems to me the colors were most satisfactory."

Michel Conan, director of garden studies at Dumbarton Oaks, believes that, so far as Bliss and Farrand were concerned, the plantings in the individual

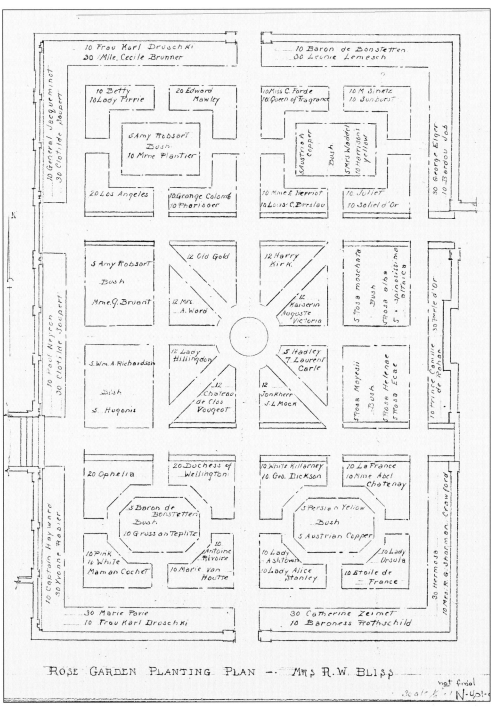

Rose Garden Planting Plan — Mrs R.W. Bliss

Top:
Superintendent William Gray and the Dumbarton Oaks garden crew, c. 1937.

Left:
A planting plan for the Rose Garden by Beatrix Farrand.

Above:
Plantings of hollyhocks along a walkway.

gardens at Dumbarton Oaks did not necessarily follow fixed plans. A good example of this is the Rose Garden. Its planting plan history was completely researched by Gail Griffin, the superintendent, prior to its being replanted in 1997. "The Rose Garden was first thought of as a *lawn* of roses," says Conan. The flower colors were planned to wash across the terrace in subtle sunset hues, changing from yellow and orange in the northern third of the garden to a yellow-salmon in the center third to pink-salmon and red in the south.

Farrand and Bliss must have discussed this color scheme at their initial meeting, for in her first letter to Bliss, Farrand summed up their conversation: "As for the colors of the rose garden . . . like you, I see a medley of soft yellows, oranges and orange-salmon colors, blacks and creamy whites, and none of that horrid shade known as *cerise* by the milliners."

Various ideas were tried to add complexity to the lawn planting, such as incorporating rose trees (or standards) into the beds to add height. Borders of white candytuft were added around the flower beds, but the terrace proved too shady, and so the borders were replanted in box *suffruticosa*. Farrand mentions, of the box, that "Nothing makes a better background for rose coloring." She continues to discuss the planting, writing that "Jasmine and honeysuckle with lilies and a general attractive floppy tangle of plants . . . will make the garden look used and lived in as quickly as possible."

Because the rose varieties needed for the color-graded lawn were at that time generally unscented hybrids, the distinctive rose perfume was incorporated into the garden by other rose varieties trained up the stone walls: Mermaid, Silver Moon, Dr. Van Fleet, Reveil Dijonnais, and Cl. Frau Karl Druschki. The garden rooms, explains Michel Conan, were always planned for experimentation: "Beatrix designed them as places for gardening, and she and Mildred were always changing the planting patterns. That is, after all, what a garden is: something . . . in a constant state of flux."

Mildred Bliss loved her plants and paid attention to their every detail. Archival photographs from the 1930s illustrate what a difference Bliss's presence made to the look of the garden. In addition, no detail of the hardscaping was too small to escape her critical eye. As a result, one of Dumbarton Oaks's greatest charms is that there is always more to be discovered, whether the variety of patterns of brick in the walk or the care lavished on each element of hardscaping. A note from Ruth Havey to Mildred Bliss included three groups of preliminary sketches for the Forsythia Arch: "One with the pediment broken, one not broken, and a third group [with] part of the pediment [recessed] to give the impression of breaking it without actually disturbing the top line . . ."

James Gray

In 1937 Beatrix Farrand turned sixty-five. "Unless you see an immediate need for me at Dumbarton, I shall probably stay on here [in California] and let Max make his very hurried trip East without me," she wrote Mildred, "[but] perhaps late December and early January are not ideal moments for outdoor gardening in Washington!"

Age and infirmity were becoming more frequent topics in their correspondence. And then, on December 31, 1937, James Gray suddenly died of a heart attack. He was only fifty-five years old. "He died as he had lived," Bliss wrote Farrand, "reasoningly, unhastily, considerately . . . I know that you have been thinking as I have, thankfully, that Gray lived to see the garden, his baby, grow up." The next spring a tribute to Gray was set into the greenhouse wall.

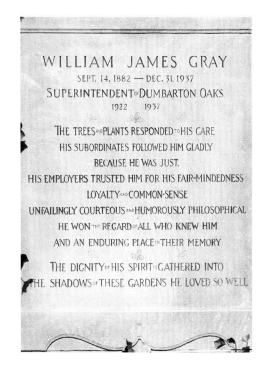

WILLIAM JAMES GRAY

SEPT. 14, 1882 — DEC. 31, 1937

SUPERINTENDENT of DUMBARTON OAKS
1922   1937

THE TREES and PLANTS RESPONDED to HIS CARE

HIS SUBORDINATES FOLLOWED HIM GLADLY

BECAUSE HE WAS JUST.

HIS EMPLOYERS TRUSTED HIM FOR HIS FAIR-MINDEDNESS

LOYALTY and COMMON-SENSE

UNFAILINGLY COURTEOUS and HUMOROUSLY PHILOSOPHICAL

HE WON the REGARD of ALL WHO KNEW HIM

AND AN ENDURING PLACE in THEIR MEMORY

THE DIGNITY of HIS SPIRIT is GATHERED INTO

THE SHADOWS of THESE GARDENS HE LOVED SO WELL

Above:
Plaque to William Gray in the greenhouse wall.

In her letter about Gray, Farrand commented to Bliss about the placement of a new sculpture gallery (to be added on the west end of the music room), "another idea of Gray's," she notes. This new gallery was an indication of the Blisses' revised plans for the future management of Dumbarton Oaks. And Bliss sent Farrand a more significant hint on March 16:

Dumbarton Oaks has entered upon a new development of the most far-reaching kind . . . when I tell you that professor Kenneth Conant of Harvard has made us two visits of three days each . . . and not only Harvard, but Princeton are interesting themselves in our future, and that we are soon to publish our first Dumbarton Oaks paper and to start on the census of early Christian and Byzantine objects in Canada and the United States, you will see that the winter has been spent to good purpose.

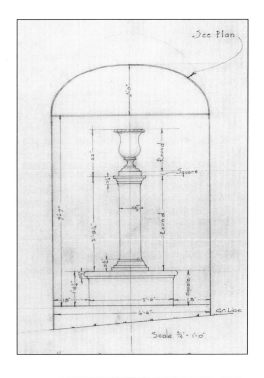

Portents of War

After Gray's death, James Bryce, a Scot on the Dumbarton Oaks gardening staff, was made head of the grounds. Bliss reports in her letter to Farrand:

Bryce has moved the trees well and quickly. Bryce, Crampton and I spent four days at the [Baltimore] Flower Show yesterday and we found no white Cyclamen or Platyclynus as good as those at Dumbarton Oaks and no Miltonia better. You will be pleased. But when I tell you there was a Cymbidium which nearly captized [sic] me with covetousness, you will be admiring—that I have kept it under control! . . .

The weeping cherries at the west end of the swimming pool are in bloom . . . Should Sunday be a fine day, I imagine it will mean a forsythia party . . .

I don't think of the misery created by the floods . . . or by Hitler and I shall be very, very glad, indeed, to see my beloved Trix again.

Farrand quickly wrote back: "All things that tend to build an enduring structure seem worth while in these days of shadow . . ." She also responded to Bliss's letter of February 10, enumerating the garden's most pressing concerns, one of which was the design of the Terrior Column. Years later, she explained the origins of the column:

[It] is a copy of one seen in a garden outside of Palermo which used to belong to the King of Naples in Nelson's time. Evidently the villa was used by British people . . . and outside the villa in the garden there was a little memorial complete with its vase with an inscription obviously carved by an Italian who knew no English, saying that the column and vase were set up in memory of a beloved terrier, which was Italianized into "terrior," hence the name.

Top:
Farrand's measured sketch of the original Terrior Column.

Above:
The original Terrior Column in Naples, Italy.

Placed throughout the garden are several specially designed seats that each have a story associated with them. Most of the garden furnishings were designed by Bliss working with either Farrand or Havey. Each seat was designed for its particular location in the garden; at Bliss's request, they were constructed out of a wide variety of materials: iron, wood, carved stone, lead, cast stone.

The seat near the Terrior Column, constructed in 1938, is a fantasy concocted between Mildred Bliss and Ruth Havey. Farrand saw a preliminary sketch of it in 1935 and wanted no part of it. She later described the seat's origins: "The iron swing . . . is merely an adaptation of some French Rococo designs and its figures were largely chosen after some engravings in an 18th century book on the zoo at Versailles where the Aesop's fables were used in the iron

Above:
The Terrior Column at Dumbarton Oaks,
installed in 1932.

work grilles which surround the cages of the animals . . ." Havey often found inspiration for her designs not in Palermo but in the illustrated books at the New York Public Library or in Bliss's own collection of garden books.

Havey showed Farrand some drawings of her and Bliss's new, more fancifully designed furniture; an elaborate letter to Bliss shows that Farrand was not pleased. "By all means let us follow your inspired idea to cut out the figures and put just aluminum painted panels inside what you kindly call 'the pretty borders,'" she tartly wrote, referring to the new Orion and Bootes chairs for the Star Garden. "And about the placement of the Unicorn Lady [purchased for $3,050 from the sculptor Daniel G. Olney]," she writes, "we will delightedly see that the lady is moved down to the two trees among the rhododendrons at the west end of the park."

Farrand added, "This brings me to the question of the cost of designing." Referring to Frederick Coles, the estate's resident sculptor, she wrote, "I find that Coles' per diem fee is $20. This makes him rather more expensive than even the expensive Miss. Havey, and I wonder whether for some of the designing such as the forsythia gate and the seat for the 'terrior' we might not do well to have the Haveylet do some of her . . . more imaginative work. Let me know about this as the Haveylet sends me better sketches to work from than does the somewhat lumbering Coles . . ."

In response to Farrand's suggestions about designers, Mildred Bliss replied, "When a really distinguished piece of designing is necessary Havey should be consulted . . . When routine work is involved, Coles can do it provided he is asked about how many day's work it will take so that we decide whether it is worth the expense or not . . ." Frederick Coles was responsible for many of the carved stone details at Dumbarton Oaks. When not busy at the estate, Coles and his brother executed the lettering for the Lincoln Memorial in Washington, D.C.

"I should want to see a batch of designs suitable for the Lilac Circle before deciding to alter what I think a particularly successful bench," Bliss wrote to Farrand. Her demanding tone, perhaps, was meant to prod Farrand back into greater participation at Dumbarton Oaks, but the designer's top priority was now her failing husband, Max.

Tributes

Mildred Bliss, busy as ever, was already into the planning for the new Study Center's opening, still two years off. She asked Royall Tyler that July if he would write the institute's first paper: "We wanted, for sheer sentient's sake, to have Dumbarton Oaks make its first bow to the reading public over your signature alone," she told him. For many years, Tyler had continued to regale Mildred with letters of his exploits and to advise her and Robert on purchases for their collections.

The Dumbarton Oaks gardens were open to the public for the first time for one day in the fall of 1938, "when the dahlias, chrysanthemums and autumn leaves are a riot of color." That fall, too, Nadia Boulanger came to Dumbarton Oaks to direct the premier of Igor Stravinsky's Concerto in E-flat, a piece that had been commissioned by the Blisses to commemorate their thirtieth wedding anniversary.

The concerto was performed in the Blisses' elegant music room, already the site of many exceptional musical events sponsored by the couple. These concerts were later continued under the stewardship of Harvard and the Friends of Music at Dumbarton Oaks. (The Friends group, formed in 1946 to ensure that music remained a part of the life of the center, still sponsors the concert series.)

Suffering from bronchitis, Farrand was not able to respond to Bliss's letters dating back to December 1938 until March 1939. Still impatient with her friend's long absence, Bliss punctiliously wrote back, not forgetting to chide Farrand for omitting to thank Henry Du Pont for some allium bulbs: "So I wrote Harry Du Pont that you were so meticulous that your note to him had gone astray. Capisce?"

In April Farrand heard from James Bryce that "The primroses were especially pretty, daffodils still good, and the stream-side still looking its best."
The maintenance for such naturalistic-looking features as the primroses was enormous. Annually 150 candelabra primroses, *Primula polyanthus* "Munstead" strain, were planted en masse along the creek. The daffodils, on the other hand, were easier. Varieties in the woodlands included both the simple yellow jonquil and *Narcissus poeticus* as well as the white Pheasant's Eye, which Farrand combined with clumps of the native *Mertensia virginiana*, or Virginia bluebells.

Mildred Bliss decided to dedicate a bench at Dumbarton Oaks to her Washington neighbors, Caroline and William Phillips. William Phillips, like Robert, served in the United States foreign service; his father, Duncan Phillips, had assembled a sensitive collection of avant-garde European and American paintings from the early decades of the twentieth century—what is known today as the Phillips Collection.

Bliss wrote of the bench to Caroline Phillips: "Please . . . be an angel and send me whatever inscription you would like on your and William's benches. As I told you in my letter last June, the big bench we always thought a failure, so we have concocted two others which make an exceedingly pretty unit and we are very anxious to get it entirely finished as soon as may be." The inscription on the bench (not chosen by Caroline Phillips, who wrote, "I hardly feel capable of choosing my own epitaph") was taken from Dante's *Divine Comedy:*

Ma con piena letizia l'ore prime,
Cantando picevieno intra le foflie che
Tenevan bordone alle sue rime.

(But with full joy singing
[the little birds] received the early breezes among the leaves,
which kept a burden to their rhyme.)

Inscriptions, occasionally inaccurately transcribed, are found throughout the garden, often chosen as tributes to specific friends. There is the plaque dedicated to Beatrix Farrand on the balcony of the Green Garden, for example. On a stone panel in the wisteria arbor of the Arbor Terrace another quote, also from the *Divine Comedy*, is dedicated to Gelasio B. A. Caetani, the Italian ambassador to the United States from 1922 to 1925, who was a close friend and frequent guest of the Blisses:

Quelli ch anticamente poetaro
Leta dell'oro
& suo stato felice
Forse in parnaso
Esto luco sognaro
Codice caetani
All amico gelaso.

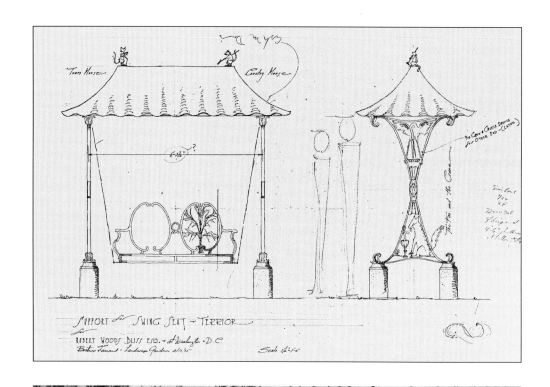

Top right:
Farrand/Havey design for the Anglo-Chinois swing seat near the Terrior Column, decorated with characters from Aesop's fables, 1935.

Above:
Armand Albert Rateau's design for a vase atop a pedestal, used with the semicircular bench dedicated to Caroline and William Phillips.

Above right:
Rateau's spare design for a semicircular bench.

Right:
Farrand's modification of Rateau's bench design, which was built about 1939.

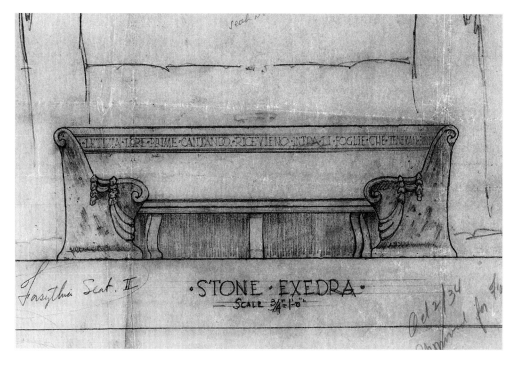

(Those who in the old time sang
of the Golden Age,
and of its happy state,
perchance, upon Parnassus,
dreamed of this place.)

The Dumbarton Oaks Study Center

On January 3, 1940, Mildred Bliss was in New York with Farrand for an initial meeting with Jack Thacher. A representative from Harvard's Fogg Museum, Thacher was soon to become the first director of the Dumbarton Oaks Study Center. He had been brought in to represent Dumbarton Oaks's new administrators as some final design decisions were discussed. Together Bliss, Farrand, and Thacher ironed out final design details concerning the inscriptions for the Forsythia Arch and for the chronological tablets. But "beyond that," Bliss told Ruth Havey, "I must turn the key on desires of this sort . . ."

January 1940 found Farrand fighting another severe cold. She had, however, managed a quick trip to Washington the previous month to tour the garden grounds with Bliss. "Dearest Trix," Bliss writes, with a surprising current of irony, "Your gallant self-discipline in making yourself work against the heavy odds of your really severe cold . . . touched me very much. Of course, no sacrifice you ever make for Dumbarton Oaks is a surprise . . ."

In May 1940, a garden party was given by the Blisses at Dumbarton Oaks in honor of the delegates to the Eighth American Scientific Congress. Reported Katherine Brooks, a local society columnist: "Foreigners were particularly interested in the variety of flowers and shrubs and few failed to take the walk down the sloping grounds . . . Amusing incidents were caused by several who were lost from their little groups." She also described the hostess:

Mrs. Bliss was dressed in a long gold-colored crepe, the skirt flaring to the hem and the gracefully draped bodice cut high in the neckline and having three-quartered-length sleeves which flared like the skirt. Her gloves were a lighter shade and were long. About her neck she wore a string of uncut jade beads, which were held apart by narrow bands in tiny diamonds, and from this hung a pendant of jade, also uncut but polished. She wore no hat and the green of the jade on the gold-colored gown brought out the rich beauty of her titian hair.

In June 1940, Max Farrand underwent more surgery. Robert Bliss, too, was still convalescing on the West Coast. Mildred, concerned for Robert, concerned for Max, concerned about the possibility of war, and concerned about the future of Dumbarton Oaks, wrote to Beatrix:

The weeks pass—agonizing weeks—and still I am unable to talk to you of whom I think so particularly often . . .

Letters are coming from France now, brought by hand mostly, and they all tell the same story. The unanimity is significant: fronte populaire, demoralization, fifth column insidious work, and astonishment on the part of the people, which was soberly ready for sacrifice and expected the leadership and equipment to beat the enemy which it did not receive from the hands of its political leaders . . .

As for me, the outer shell of me is all right. I seem to be in a period of complete lucidity, which is helpful, and I get in some sixteen hours' work a day, which isn't enough. However, the new [museum wing] will soon be rid of its workmen and, after a week's air-conditioning, books and cases will go in. We shall definitely be ready for the University and the public in October ... The following is a most appropriate and beautiful quotation from Meander which we will put on the frieze of the Loggia in the cortile instead of the names of the five Emperors:

"Art is for men a refuge from sorrow."

A New Outpost

"Whether you pronounce BIZ-an-tin or bee-ZAN-tine, the Byzantine atmosphere has injected itself with a bang into the current Capital scene," Hope Ridings Miller wrote in the *Washington Post* on Sunday, November 2, 1940. She continued:

Credit for the reversion to a dark and dead past here on the eve of the Presidential election goes to Mr. and Mrs. Robert Woods Bliss, whose research library and medieval objects of art were viewed by a large number of notables on Friday night and are being discussed at four conferences at Dumbarton Oaks this weekend ...

Indeed, the whirl of lectures, luncheons and dinners has become so exciting that diplomats are talking more about the "Bliss-krieg" than anything else these days, and more than one book on medieval art has been hauled out and patiently perused by Capitalites who want to keep up their end of the conversation.

The *Times-Herald* followed up with an announcement the next day, noting that the Blisses were giving the administration of the estate to Harvard University: "'Dumbarton Oaks is now ready to increase its contribution to the intellectual life of the nation,' Mr. Bliss said."

Bernard Berenson sent a telegram: "Full of admiration for your Noble and fascinating achievement ..." Joseph Alsop wrote: "The festival Dumbarton was ... particularly happy in such times as these. So much of value is being destroyed ... that it meant much to see a new outpost, fortified with all the artillery of beauty and learning in which the good life may be defiantly and securely lived." And commented Beatrix Farrand: "To you and Robert it must be like the marrying off of a child—content of the future & what it holds, and just a little chokey for the present."

In November 1940 Max Farrand made the announcement that, after fourteen years, he would be stepping down as director of the Huntington Art Gallery and Library. Mildred Bliss sent a telegram to Beatrix: "How strange our parallel decision should unite us so closely these very days." On December 1 of the same year, the Washington *Times-Herald* announced:

Bliss Estate Transferred to Harvard
$1,300,000 Gift to Serve as Park, Research Center
Most of the Robert Woods Bliss estate, valued at more than $1,300,000, has been donated to the United States and Harvard University for a public park and cultural research center, the National Capital Park and Planning Commission officially announced yesterday.

The former ambassador and his wife, Mrs. Mildred B. Bliss, have signed two deeds, it was announced, one of them turning over to the Government 27 acres of the estate ... to be included in Washington's park system as a beauty spot and recreation center open to the public.

The other deed gives 16¼ acres, including the magnificent Georgian mansion . . . , a treasure house of art objects, to Harvard University to be used as a research unit . . .

While it is true that the Blisses had conceived of Dumbarton Oaks as a center for scholars from the very beginning, they had always intended to turn it over to an institution to administer following their deaths. What changed in 1940, Mildred Bliss later commented, was the scare of another war: "We felt that inevitably the United States would be drawn into the conflict [and] sensing that the war would change the whole pattern of our lives, we decided to realize our plans for Dumbarton Oaks during our lifetime."

Farrand had not spent a great deal of time on site at Dumbarton Oaks since 1938; Ruth Havey, tentatively, had filled the void. But with Dumbarton Oaks being administered by Harvard University and her husband retiring, Beatrix Farrand was keen to be a part of the center's new life. By mid-January, she had met in Washington with the center's new director, Jack Thacher, and Professor Sach of Harvard. She wired to Mildred: "They seemed to feel that visit had latent useful possibilities."

Farrand was back, and she wasted no time in sending in her first report on the gardens, dated February 17. For fourteen years the director's wife at the Huntington, she knew first-hand the problems that could arise when a public institution takes over a private dwelling. In order to guide the new owners of Dumbarton Oaks, she began to prepare a garden planting record book as a permanent account of the rationale behind the development of the various gardens' schemes.

Within less than a year, the peripatetic Blisses were beginning to confound Jack Thacher. Farrand wrote to Anne Sweeney:

You and I both know what a busy pair of Chiefs we are dealing with, and it will make you laugh when you hear that Mr. Thacher came over to see me [at Reef Point] with regard to Dumbarton Oaks affairs and looked at me in utter astonishment because he had received no answer to a long letter full of questions addressed to either Mr. or Mrs. Bliss . . . I told him, with nearly as straight face as possible, that he need in no way worry himself as . . . I had sometimes to wait months for an important answer, or go ahead and do the thing and take the responsibility for it.

Energized by her new position of authority, Farrand kept up her correspondence not only with Bliss, Sweeney, and Havey, but with Thacher, Coles, and Bryce. A letter from Farrand in September 1941 brought Bliss up to date:

You will smile grimly when you hear that I have spent a very considerable amount of time trying to shorten your chronological historical tablet, as your inscription totals about 180 words which is an immense number to arrange without crowding on one stone. By extreme care and much thought and considerable time I have managed to cut two words out which I think will have to go back! . . .

The terrior seat should by this time be nearly ready, and Coles wrote me that when not too hot, he was also working on the Mother-of-Pearl fountain . . .

The "Mother-of-Pearl fountain" is not a fountain at all, but a trompe l'oeil plaque. Its stylized perspective design of a latticed alcove with an inlaid mother-of-pearl water spray at its center was to be positioned at the end of the walk next to the Lilac Circle. Such a perspective play is a common garden device that disguises the abrupt ending of a path.

Once the United States had entered the war, Dumbarton Oak's collections were placed in storage for safekeeping, development on the new Study Center was curtailed, and the gardening staff was cut by half; plantings were simplified or, in instances like the vegetable garden, simply done away with altogether. Worried about Farrand's delicate health, Bliss wrote to her: "Before stepping over into other realms [the planting record book], won't you please, Trix darling, tell me if you yourself are all right or if this whole difficult year has been too much for you."

Mildred Bliss was still spending much time on the West Coast keeping Robert company during his long convalescence. She kept busy. Music, Herr Siposs, gardens, and the situation abroad were her priorities, and she continued her mother's example by assisting with the development of the Santa Barbara Botanical Garden, securing Farrand's opinions when needed. She herself was not shy about giving advice, as in a letter she wrote to the wife of Jascha Heifetz, the famous violinist:

Dear Mrs. Heifetz,
The Brahms and Schubert are still ringing in my happy memory of a delightful four hours of oblivion to the miseries which fill one's thoughts these dreadful months . . .

Would you be kind enough to give the enclosed card to the Ratoffs, who said they were coming to Santa Barbara for a thinning cure. As there is nobody better in the entire country for conditioning than Siposs, who has been our trainer for ten years and who came to this country because of us, I should like to give them his address. If ever you or Heifetz need any building up or rebuilding after an illness, this man is nothing short of a wizard . . .

The Scholars Move In

How was Dumbarton Oaks after its first year with Harvard? Reporter John White tried to find out in the *Times-Herald* on November 30, 1941:

A remarkable thing happened here a year ago. The Blisses moved out and the scholars moved in.

Appointed for a year . . . these scholars (most of them not Harvard educated) were given board and lodging and study rooms and access to priceless, ever-increasing source-material.

With only rudimentary restrictions, their time was their own. Their subject for study was their own . . . For the scholars the setup must have resembled heaven.

There is nothing like it in this country. And (even before the war) nothing like it anywhere else in the world, except possibly the American Academy in Rome. Well, a year has passed. How has it been? The answer to that is this: Go and see for yourself . . .

In mid-May Bliss excitedly wrote Farrand: "We are, at last, definitely going eastward . . . Therefore, HOW? WHEN? WHERE?," she asks, would they meet at Dumbarton Oaks.

The happy meeting took place in June, but unfortunately, Farrand suddenly fell ill and was compelled to return at once to Reef Point. Bliss, however, with her usual vitality, quickly resumed her former pace upon returning to Washington. With Farrand's assistance, she had prepared three sets of notes:

Above:
The "Mother-of-Pearl" fountain along the
west border near the Lilac Circle.

one on Dumbarton Oaks Park, another concerning Dumbarton Oaks proper, and a two-page agenda of items to discuss with both superintendent James Bryce and director Jack Thacher. The agenda included such observations as "The Bride magnolia was in excellent condition, better [for the pruning] than in several years past . . . The iris garden was much curtailed on account of the infected soil which had destroyed many of the iris. The cherry trees [beneath which the iris was planted] show infinitely better above the plain green lawn but one misses the beauty of the iris . . ." Plainly, nothing escaped Bliss's notice.

Prepared by Jack Thacher, the official transcript of that meeting between Bliss, Bryce, and himself ends with the note: "Suggest to Mrs. Bliss a possibility of Miss. Havey being the replacer of B.F. when B.F. retires." Later that fall, Thacher reflected upon what had prompted this thought: Beatrix Farrand's unexpected departure the previous June, owing to ill health. "Before Mrs. Farrand left I had several conversations with her regarding the possibility of a successor," he wrote. Farrand herself had begun to think about retirement. In June 1942 she had turned seventy-three. She wrote to Mildred Bliss:

My very dearest . . . To keep the balance between integrated work and over-fatigue is not an easy lesson but I am trying to do it and so far with considerable success. Leaving Dumbarton Oaks was of course a hard knock as it was the first time I had to confess myself beaten [a reference to her absence in 1940] . . .

The work with Miss. Havey in the last few days shows that she promises well. As you and I know she needs guidance as the experience and maturity of judgement are quite naturally missing, but for the Dumbarton work there seems no one as immediately promising, and as she has made herself well liked by those with whom she works she would seem to me, as before suggested, the logical person, provided she is willing to give the time and learn what she must learn before she can adequately replace the hands that have for so long been alongside yours on the reins . . . Really things go better—medico quite satisfied & wants me to go on but not under super heated high pressure steam!

Although Farrand wrote of stepping back, the chief difference in her involvement would be that, instead of visiting the garden herself, the garden—or rather those who sought her advice—would now travel to her, either in Bar Harbor, New Haven, or New York City, where she still maintained her offices. In June 1942 Farrand wired Bliss from New Haven: "Haveylet and I earnestly working over inscription and vista."

But Max Farrand, still not well, underwent an operation for cancer of the bladder. The Blisses, meanwhile, had sold the Casa Dorinda. In 1942 both couples spent the winter in Montecito at the Valley Club.

In the spring, as she wended her way east, Farrand stopped in Philadelphia to receive a medal from the Garden Club of America in New York. She stayed for four days in Washington, D.C. In April 1943, in addition to her work at Dumbarton Oaks, Farrand would also redesign the garden at the Blisses' new house: "Bryce tells me you find the garden a little over-elaborate, which of course is true . . . Just as a matter of manners, I am writing a note to Miss. Rose Greeley, who designed the garden . . . I hope she will not think I am doing professional violence to her design."

Robert Bliss had found the new house on 28th Street, just a few blocks around the corner from Dumbarton Oaks. Mildred, who never liked the place, referred disdainfully to it as "the shack." But Robert had returned to

Washington to assist at the state department, and there had not been a lot of time for house-hunting.

Dumbarton Oaks, too, was making its own contribution to the war effort. Robert Bliss explained the situation that April before the Harvard Club:

The end of May last year Mrs. Bliss and I were much gratified when a considerable portion of [Dumbarton Oaks] was turned over to the National Defense Research Committee, and Dumbarton Oaks found itself making a definite contribution to war work . . . One half of the building is devoted to evolving means to kill human beings more speedily and in greater numbers; the other half continues to develop greater knowledge of the artistic creation of man. One works for the development of the most hideous activity of war, the other for the discovery and preservation of the beauty of human expression.

As World War II began to wind down, Dumbarton Oaks made another contribution. On July 24, 1944, an item appeared in the *Washington Daily News:*

There was a time when an invitation there was the epitome of social success. The hostess, a great beauty, with magnificent figure, Titian hair, perfectly gowned, and always wearing pale lemon-colored suede gloves, received her friends in the huge drawing room of Washington's most beautiful home . . .

Now a new era of history begins for Dumbarton Oaks. The dons and researchers of Harvard University will make way . . . for the delegates of the four-power post-war security conferences to be held here in August.

The *Washington Star* commented on the Dumbarton Oaks meetings on August 1:

"Peace" is the watchword of the conference, and if the delegates [from the United States, Great Britain, China, and Russia] are influenced by their environment it should be a success. No more peaceful atmosphere than the walled-in acres of the estate, with its giant oaks, sloping lawns, formal gardens and tiled swimming pool, around the banks of which cushioned lounge chairs recline in the shade of a vine-covered wall . . .

The Dumbarton Oaks conference on postwar security, held at the estate in the summer of 1944, paved the way for the establishment of the UNO or, as it is now known, the United Nations.

Beatrix Farrand relentlessly continued working for Dumbarton Oaks. In August Bliss received the first draft of Farrand's monumental *Plant Book* and gratefully responded: "This, it seems to me, is of such importance in its detail, not only for the future of Dumbarton Oaks, but also in its principles for all landscape gardeners . . . It would be difficult for me to tell you how grateful I am for it and how much I appreciate the labor it has involved for you."

Farrand's *Plant Book* is a remarkable document because it explains the thought processes behind each of the decisions made in the garden: why each area was designed as it was, and how and with what plants each effect then was achieved. The book has been an invaluable help in the maintenance and restoration of Dumbarton Oaks.

Max Farrand died at Reef Point in June 1945. "The last years have taken their toll of energy and resistance and now I am a tired old woman," Beatrix Farrand wrote to Bliss the following April. "There is nothing the matter, no physical gear out of order, but not much strength and great weariness."

Nevertheless, Farrand arranged to meet with Jack Thacher in Boston to discuss the maintenance of the gardens, now that the war had ended. She informed Bliss: "[Jack Thacher and I] are both deeply concerned about the condition at Dumbarton Oaks . . . it needs trained care and rehabilitation after the necessarily scant war years . . . I am no longer strong enough to ramp up & down those hills as we used to . . . [however] Mr. Thacher seems flatteringly unwilling to drop me completely."

On May 15 Beatrix Farrand suggested a plan whereby Robert Patterson, a landscape architect and engineer who was assisting her at Reef Point and the Arnold Arboretum, where Farrand was now a consulting landscape gardener, could act as her surrogate. It was arranged that Patterson spend three days in May at Dumbarton Oaks; Farrand stated that he would "need the time to absorb as much as possible of Oakdum in order to report to me his conclusions." Clearly, she meant to continue her oversight of Dumbarton Oaks—in spirit if not in person.

Robert Patterson wrote to Jack Thacher following the tour: "I have had several talks with Mrs. Farrand . . . My first and most recurrent reaction was that the luxuriance of the place is somewhat overpowering, and that the design is becoming a little obscured in places." (He admits, however, that the shock of coming from bleak early-spring Maine to early-summer Washington could account for some of that "overpowering" impression.) Patterson continued, "There are two elements which seemed to me to need very careful study: the West Lawn and the North Vista . . ."

Bliss found it difficult to accept Farrand's now near total absence, and simply chose to ignore it. She wrote to Farrand on July 26, 1946, including a typically thorough list of questions and comments:

I went over your June 11th letter with Thacher and would like to take up the following points with you . . . Paragraph 3: Agreed that Orchard, Star, and Crabapple Hill planting should be thinned. In regard to the Orangery, I do not agree that because it is used as much it should be more "impersonal," as you suggest. It is precisely this "personal" characteristic which makes Dumbarton Oaks what it is, and wherever that element can be combined with practical workableness it should in our opinion be retained . . . We don't agree that the little brick ribbon running down the Melisande's Allee should be widened, but we do completely agree that the Goat Trail [the walk across Crabapple Hill] should be made safe for elderly knees and careless ankles . . . Can't the overgrown white Azalea from the Star Garden be used north of the Swimming Pool? . . . I am not at all sure that added paved space is necessary south and north of the middle doors of the Orangery. This is not where most people congregate. I think Bryce and Sweeney know more about the public habits than you, Mr. Patterson, Robert or I, and I would go very piano indeed on changing the design of that part . . .

Common Work, Common Delight

Farrand, seventy-four years old, was keenly feeling Max's loss and the fact of her own mortality. She wrote to Mildred Bliss in October 1946:

You may have forgotten that you were told that the small oil Odilon Redon which hung in the library at the Pavillon Colombe was coming to you and on to Dumbarton later.

It is far more fun to send it to you now and to know that you and Robert will enjoy it, without waiting for me to disappear from the horizon . . .

Edith enjoyed the picture, and I bought it from her estate, so the history is complete.

For four days in February 1947, Mildred Bliss, Jack Thacher, Robert Patterson, Anne Sweeney, and James Bryce met at Dumbarton Oaks to compile a complete tally of the gardens, the first such thorough review since the beginning of the war. The result, a five-page report, covered every section of the grounds: steps, walks and drains; greenhouses; budgets and issues of the handling of visitors in the garden. The library and other technical data were growing, exceeding the allotted space in the Catalog House; the idea of building a new garden library was proposed (the suggestion was made that the new library replace the Orangery, but that idea was dropped). Bliss sent Farrand a full report, "You will, I feel sure . . . make Dumbarton a visit in the Spring, we should then be able to decide definitively what is to be done."

Robert Patterson was beginning to feel hemmed in by Farrand's overarching authority. "I have not said anything to Mrs. Farrand about the idea of blotting out the North Vista with trees," he told Jack Thacher, "[but] I do feel that some kind of planting would be a great help."

Even from the distance of Reef Point, Farrand sensed the dual undercurrents of Bliss's continued dependence upon her and Patterson's desire for a freer hand. On February 28, with Bliss's "encyclopedic" letter to one side and "Mr. Patterson's full report" of the February meeting to the other, Farrand lamented:

The two together propound so many problems that I find myself overwhelmed, and because of this sense of bewilderment and lack of strength, a long latent decision seems wise to make at once. It is perfectly clear that . . . there is no likelihood of my ever really being strong again . . . So it will be kinder to Dumbarton and wiser for the rest of us to face the fact that after a happy association with its loveliness, I must give up the idea of advising and counseling and probably further visits.

Making this decision is a good deal like tearing off an arm or a leg or cutting out one's heart, but the change has got to come some day and Dumbarton develop on lines that I might not be able to approve or follow.

Distressed by Farrand's resignation—and bewildered, as if it had come out of the blue—Bliss immediately wrote to Jack Thacher asking for a copy of Patterson's garden report. She wanted to review it herself before responding to Farrand. "I read it and thought it a meticulously accurate resume of [our] 'thinking aloud' discussions, which is just what we all feel is due you and what you would expect of his loyalty," Bliss wrote to her. She answered each of Farrand's objections in an effort to explain away her concerns:

Not a decision—or even a near one—was reached, even in principle, regarding the Orangery, which, as it happens, we all want to keep! Also, dear, in your second paragraph page one you say that Patterson's and my letters "together propose so many problems" etc., and on re-reading my letter I find only mentioned one subject regarding Dumbarton Oaks—the Herbaceous Border—and at that, only one short paragraph of speculative musing! . . .

If you have decided irrevocably that you must retire, then of course, you must write to Mr. Thacher, who felt very real personal regret when I read him bits of your letter to me . . .

Above:
Odilon Redon, Vase of Flowers,
c. 1910, once in the collection of Edith Wharton and presented to the Blisses by Beatrix Farrand.

You also write you "must give up the idea of advising and counseling and probably of further visits." Now that, Trix dear, we cannot accept, any of us. You owe it to Dumbarton Oaks, to Harvard and to Thacher to bring your professional relationship to a graceful close. And what of us? Of Robert and me? I simply refuse to believe that you would so deeply hurt our affections.

So I hope you will arrange to spend two spring days in your third floor room [at Dumbarton] . . . and I will limit our little visits with you as strictly as you wish.

Good night Trix darling. Let us hear from you before too long. My devoted affection enfolds you, Mildred

Bliss's careful and thorough explanation reassured her friend, but in fact, Farrand's decision had been long overdue, however difficult it was for them both to accept. Farrand, in her reply to Bliss's appeal, confided that, even when her retirement was to go into effect on June 30, Jack Thacher nevertheless

would like me to continue to counsel and aid from the point of "remote control" of emerita . . . So apparently those whom I love at Dumbarton Oaks still want my elderly finger in the pie.

Thank you for so many hours of common work, and common delight, the spring days and summer evenings full of thrush song and moonlight, and the autumn days of color and blue skies.

Above:
Beatrix Farrand at Reef Point,
c. 1950.

Autumn

Previous pages:
Shield with wheat sheaf and oak leaves at
the back of the Quod Severis Metes bench in
the Rose Garden; view north toward Rock
Creek Park from the Arbor Terrace balcony.

Top:
Crab apples in the orchard.

Above:
View west through the Herbaceous Border.

Opposite:
Asters and chrysanthemums in the
Herbaceous Border.

Top:
The Beech Terrace.

Above:
Typical lead and carved-stone ornament.

Opposite:
View from the Box Walk to the Ellipse.

Following pages:
The Fountain Terrace.

Above, clockwise from top left:
Chrysanthemums on the Fountain Terrace;
porcelain berry on the wall of the Fountain
Terrace; autumn chrysanthemums;
chrysanthemum flowers and columbine
leaves.

Opposite:
Kearny Baldacchino on the Fountain
Terrace.

Following pages:
View north from the Fountain Terrace;
view of the Pebble Pool from the Green
Garden with vase ornament designed by
Beatrix Farrand about 1932.

Chapter Six: 1947–1969

The "Report on Dumbarton Oaks Garden Tours" of April 5 through June 29, 1947, tallied 17,198 visitors for the season. Once Beatrix Farrand's regime of "enforced rest and idleness" was "beginning to bear fruit," she was again writing faithfully to Mildred Bliss about Dumbarton Oaks, a subject to which, despite her resolutions, she always returned.

Farrand mentions a new plan to Bliss, one that would allow Dumbarton Oaks to serve its community "as no other place has." She wrote:

This implies more than actual gardens—it means a reading room where current and useful magazines, catalogues and books may be freely consulted, a small but well-chosen collection of really first-rate books on the development of the art of gardening . . . [which] should be supported by prints, monographs, and plans of well-designed gardens . . . The student would gain and could consult not only books covering local and present conditions, but the foundation books and prints underlying garden philosophy and design.

Bliss was captivated with the idea, so much in line with the plans for a new Garden Library—and it might keep Farrand engaged at Dumbarton Oaks. Within weeks Bliss mailed several book lists to Farrand for her approval, noting, "There is at the moment nobody with any knowledge of the garden books . . . I shall be more than grateful for your help and counsel." Beatrix Farrand was, after all, the perfect adviser for the project; she had been collecting garden books and prints since her twenties, and she continued to canvass the rare book sellers' lists as she rounded out her own library at Reef Point.

Robert Patterson and Jack Thacher may secretly have hoped that they were free of the demanding Farrand. But Patterson reported to Thacher in August that the "subject of the moment is the Garden Center, about which Mrs. Farrand and Mrs. Bliss have had a good deal of correspondence. Both are off, vent a terre, on a hunt for books, both rare and otherwise." He adds in script at the bottom of the letter: "Mrs. F. is ill again—lumbago & general depression. May or may not visit D.O. this year."

Beatrix Farrand's depression could not have been helped when, in the fall of 1947, a fire swept Bar Harbor, decimating whole sections of the village. Reef Point was entirely spared, but some of Farrand's work on the island, in particular sections of the landscaping she had designed along the carriage roads in Acadia National Park, was destroyed.

The letters between Bliss and Farrand, frequent and fervent as ever, now largely dealt with bibliographic matters. In the spring of 1948, Farrand scored a coup by purchasing "the entire output of Gertrude Jekyll's long and distinguished career"—a collection of plans, working drawings, and accompanying letters—for her own collection at Reef Point.

In response to Farrand's query about the purchase of some Redoute prints, Bliss joked, "I should like nothing better than to raid the Morgan Library! [But] plainly, I shall go to my grave unsatisfied, as I should like the entire collection in the original bindings, and as it is most unlikely that such a scoop as that . . . will ever befall me, I shall have to console myself with half measures and second bests."

Revitalized by the end of the war, and now back in Washington and living just around the corner from Dumbarton Oaks, Bliss was starting to get new thoughts about the garden itself. She hinted to Jack Thacher that redesigns were in order and that she might even bring Ruth Havey back for a "bang-up finale." Clearly, she had caught her second wind.

Patterson continued to oversee Dumbarton Oaks, but the sticky question of what to do with the North Vista persisted. "I am still trying to get at [Farrand's] files to see what is available in the way of old drawings for the final elements on the North Vista wall," he wrote to Jack Thacher in April 1948. In October, Patterson reported that "Mrs. Farrand has, of her own accord, made the Great Suggestion: that the north wall of the North Vista be completely removed. She has seen the plan for the walks and the new platform outside the north end, and after thinking it over, reached the same conclusion that we did, that the north wall would be in the way."

Ruth Havey

In July 1949 James Bryce retired after almost a decade as superintendent of the gardens. He was replaced by a member of the garden crew, Matthew Kearney, a native of Kerry, Ireland, who had begun his garden training at the Letchworth Nurseries in Herteford, England.

The year 1949 saw the return of Ruth Havey. By July she was sufficiently far along with one of Bliss's new schemes to tell her that "The model for the Melisande Steps is finished—not an exhibition piece—but a good solid contraption and portable . . . I will shepherd it to Washington." This entirely new design, for a feature that was planned to be installed at the bottom of Mélisande's Allée, was a fanciful rococo console with enormous stone snails as its major decorative motif. (The snails may have been a reference to André Le Nôtre. He once joked that his own coat-of-arms should consist of three snails surrounding a spade atop a cabbage leaf.)

The "fixed parts" of Havey's model, the stone wall and steps, she explains, "are built solidly in wood and plaster, [while] the parts we want to design, like the sides of the steps and the splay of the wall and the seat, are done in clay so that we can change them around as much as we like." The design was carried quite far—the elements were carved in stone—before the project was dropped. Elements of the design were later incorporated into a wall on the North Vista.

When Dumbarton Oaks was given to Harvard, changes were made to certain elements in the garden to adapt them for public use. "Some of the 'bones' of the design, originally built of plant material, [were] made more permanent in masonry and iron," Mildred Bliss explained. Gravel paths were converted "by cementing gravel into a 'mosaic,'" turf steps were remade in red brick, and on the Herb Terrace, something more showy than a central panel of grass lawn was called for. Havey gamely responded to another of Bliss's new ideas: "The more I visualize a largish sundial of some sort on the ground in the arbor garden and the rest of the space gravel or paving—the more I delve into the subject of telling the time by the sun—the more I like the picture."

The Blisses vacationed in France that summer. From the Hotel Ritz in Paris, Mildred Bliss wrote to Robert Patterson in August: "I have worked relentlessly in straightening out the various projects I have at heart for the Dumbarton Oaks gardens." Her primary goal, however, was to get the garden back into proper shape after the lean war years.

Bliss responded to some of Havey's drawings, agreeing to go ahead with almost all of the projects: the Terrior Seat, the Finalities Tablet, the panels for the Arbor Terrace wall, and with some reservations, the Mélisande Steps, of which she wrote: "Just as soon as the right specification and estimate are accepted you must go ahead and execute this unit . . . It is so pretty that I am very much hoping a way can be found to have it built, and already passe by next summer."

Above:
Ruth Havey, c. 1920.

One of the visitors to Dumbarton Oaks that autumn was Henry F. Du Pont, the creator of the vast Winterthur gardens in Delaware. Du Pont afterward wrote to Mildred Bliss of having spent "a peaceful Sunday morning walking around the grounds . . . You have an absolutely unique collection of garden benches, [which could be] a real inspiration for many people." That thought had always been a part of Bliss's garden plan; she had gradually assembled an unequaled assortment of furniture in the garden, a collection planned to illustrate to the public ideas about the variety of materials and assortment of styles possible in garden furnishings.

Meanwhile Farrand, as consultant to the Arnold Arboretum, had discovered that Harvard was attempting "to break the provisions of Prof. [Charles Sprague] Sargent's will" by doing the unthinkable: moving his library away from the Arboretum to Cambridge. She asked Bliss, "Have you done anything yet to insure the garden center not being gobbled up by Harvard and gradually be taken away from Dumbarton Oaks?" At the same time at Reef Point, Farrand was arranging for all of her Dumbarton Oaks drawings and plans to be "packed and dispatched" down to Washington. "Few places have so long a carefully kept record of attempts, accomplishments and failures," she reminded Bliss. "For the art of landscape . . . they should be kept safely, catalogued and protected."

Farrand was then thoroughly disheartened by Harvard's actual removal of Sargent's materials from the Arboretum. Again in May she prodded Bliss: "Much of my heart lies at Oakdom, and it will not rest until you have formed some plan to prevent its being dismembered and destroyed in a comparatively short time. Too much has been lost in the wars in England and elsewhere so that Dumbarton must remain if at all humanly possible." Bliss replied that she did understand: "I am constantly alert, far from reassured, . . . [but] I am determined to win my point on autonomy [for Dumbarton Oaks]."

In July the Dumbarton Oaks Garden Library, housed in Mildred Bliss's elegant paneled drawing room, officially opened its doors. Lawrence Grant White, Robert W. Patterson, and Ruth W. Havey were the first visitors to sign their names in the guest book. A view through the trees had been cut to create a new "line of vision" from the North Vista into Dumbarton Oaks Park in the fall of 1949. Robert Bliss pronounced the change "an extreme improvement."

By spring, Ruth Havey was drawing up what everyone hoped would be the final resolution to the North Vista problem. But by early summer Robert Patterson was astonished to find that Havey and Mildred Bliss were no longer sure that the agreed-upon North Vista plan was the right one. In September Bliss broke the deadlock. "All things considered," she wrote Havey, "I personally like the view from the North Bay to be concentrated and contained [as it was in the agreed-upon North Vista design]. Although it is not *your* first choice . . . I am very glad to feel that you like it and can wholeheartedly bring it to a realization."

January 1951 found Beatrix Farrand finally closing the door on Dumbarton Oaks. She regretfully informed Mildred Bliss: "[Doctors'] orders are orders and must be obeyed. So I shall no longer be available for consultation, or even for book buying." But work still proceeded at Dumbarton Oaks. That spring the stonework on the North Vista was at last completed and, wrote Jack Thacher, "to my eyes looks well."

The final plan for the North Vista, credited to Robert Patterson, involved the building of stone walls down the sides of the lawn. The walls are angled to form a slight V—a perspective trick that makes the distance appear longer

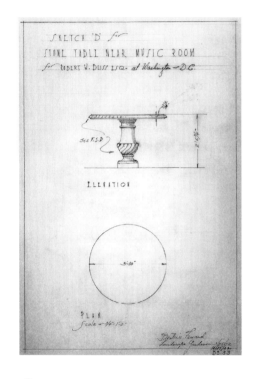

Above:
A table designed by Farrand in 1933 and sculpted by Frederick Coles.

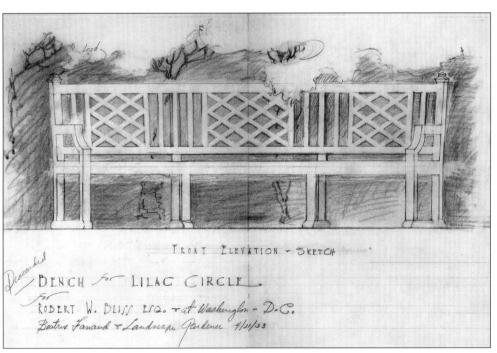

FRONT ELEVATION - SKETCH

BENCH for LILAC CIRCLE.

for
ROBERT W. BLISS ESQ. ~ at Washington ~ D.C.
Beatrix Farrand ~ Landscape Gardener 4/21/33

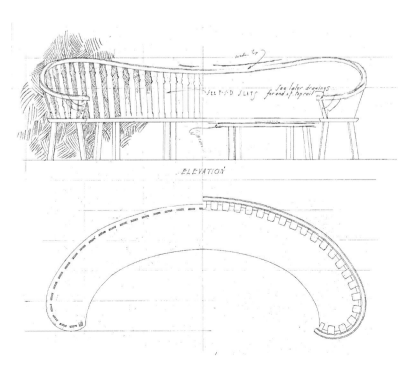

ELEVATION

Left:
Ruth Havey's console ornament for the North Vista wall, featuring decorative snails.

Center:
A wooden bench at the foot of Mélisande's Allée, designed by Farrand in 1933 after a 1929 design by Armand Albert Rateau.

Bottom:
Farrand's design for the Kidney Seat, 1931.

Top:
The Arbor Bench on the Goat Trail.

Above:
Donald Smith, superintendent of the grounds at Dumbarton Oaks, c. 1960.

Top right:
The North Vista planted in box, c. 1929.

Above right:
A mock-up of a proposed design for the North Vista, c. 1950.

Right:
The North Vista in 1959.

than it actually is. Pillars were built atop these low walls; iron chain catenaries, along which ropes of wisteria would be trained, hung between them.

New Projects

Mildred Bliss had begun a push with Harvard to establish a research fellowship in landscape gardening at Dumbarton Oaks, similar to those that already had been set up for the Byzantine and pre-Columbian scholars. With the North Vista finally nearing completion, she was eager, too, for new projects for the garden, including the construction of a new garden library wing; a garden for the blind, strong on scented and textural plants; and a Byzantine garden. She summed up her proposals in a letter to the provost of Harvard. By the next spring, she wrote, "You will find the Dumbarton Oaks Gardens rendering useful service to many categories of human being: The Blind, The Seeing, The Creative Artist, and the Research Gardener."

Robert Patterson was unconvinced. What, he asked Jack Thacher, would a fellow in garden studies actually do at Dumbarton Oaks, who would select them, who would supervise their work? As for the garden for the blind, he had practical concerns: "How are the Blind to get to the garden and get out?" He was equally unenthusiastic about the Byzantine garden, and neither of these last two schemes was ever completed.

In February 1952 Robert Patterson recommended that Donald Smith, about to graduate from the University of Maine with a degree in horticulture, be hired at Dumbarton Oaks. A native of Bar Harbor, he had worked for Beatrix Farrand at Reef Point as a teenager. Smith would become superintendent of the grounds in 1953, when Matthew Kearney retired.

For Mildred Bliss the winter had been "singularly complicated," she wrote to Farrand. She and Robert were staying at the Greenbriar, in White Sulphur Springs, Virginia, where Robert was again convalescing. But, she added, her plans for the new garden library and for the garden fellowships were going well. Meanwhile, Farrand finally cleared out her office in Bar Harbor and sent Bliss her notes for the *Plant Book*, signaling the end of her involvement with Dumbarton Oaks. She closed her letter to Bliss: "What a good time we had making our garden pudding."

In 1953 Ruth Havey was working on a design for two pairs of elaborate and massive iron and gold-leafed bronze gates for the R Street entrances. A large gilt wheat sheaf, the Bliss family emblem, crowned the gates; the design also incorporated oak leaves and acorns, representative of Dumbarton Oaks. Jack Thacher pronounced Havey's design for the gates "excellent," and so construction went ahead at a total estimated cost of twenty thousand dollars.

By this time, planting on the North Vista was finished, and it was time for the last elements of hardscaping to be installed. A bill from R. B. Phelps Cut Stone, of May 1953, gives some idea of the costs: four stone caps for the top of the gate piers cost $575 each; two consoles "cut, carved and erected" for the North Court wall totaled $1,960; the lyre consoles for the north end of the North Vista Cedar Terrace added $1,450.

The year 1953 was another difficult one. For the Blisses, it marked the passing of Mildred and Robert's old friend Royall Tyler. Royall Tyler had had a varied career: art historian, lieutenant in the U.S. Army during World War I, financial adviser first in Hungary and then with the World Bank in Paris. Lately he had been the director of the Free Europe College in Strasbourg.

He and his son William's family had remained very close to the Blisses. Through all those years, from 1902 until his death, Royall Tyler had advised Mildred and Robert on purchases for their collections, and their dream of a research center. Once in the 1960s, Mildred Bliss was asked, by the historian Walter Muir Whitehead, about the creation of Dumbarton Oaks; he wrote that she simply smiled and said, "Why you know. It was all Royall, of course."

The Blisses spent much of that year traveling. Ruth Havey kept Mildred Bliss up to date on new projects. In January 1954 she wrote:

I hardly know where to start. Every time I see [the new gates for R Street] I get so excited about them ... That man Freund [the metalworker in Astoria, New York, who built the gates] is so adroit ... He does not go off on tangents but takes the drawings of what you want and interprets it in metal in the most pleasant way. We reached the half-way mark in December and are now in the process of assembling. Thousands of little scrolls have been made—nice ones— the frame is ready to assemble—the foliage is done except for the wheat, and that is well along ...

But what pleases me most—the thing that gives me grey hairs until I see it taking shape—is that I think we have hit the right scale in choice of iron sizes. I feel satisfied now that the gates will look substantial without being clumsy.

Each of Havey's substantial-but-not-clumsy gates weighed two tons; they were installed at the R Street entrance to Dumbarton Oaks in spring 1954.

The Blisses paid a surprise call on Beatrix Farrand at Reef Point that spring. "I really think it did Mrs. Farrand a great deal of good," wrote Jack Thacher to Robert Patterson, but he added that Farrand was still very depressed. Early in 1955 she made a drastic decision: to abandon Reef Point, destroy its gardens, and have her beloved house demolished. Wrote Patterson:

There was no financial necessity for Mrs. Farrand to give up the Reef Point project, since she could have endowed it with enough funds to carry on very respectably ... I think there are many reasons for her change of heart, and it is hard to say that any one thing was responsible. She is discouraged about the future of Bar Harbor and the kind of people who are coming here, and also the difficulty of finding competent and well trained people to work on the place. I think it is also probably, although she would never say so, that she found it harder and harder to think of Reef Point without her.

Patterson purchased the Reef Point property from Farrand "with the thought of gaining a little time," hoping that some solution to stave off the garden's ultimate destruction could be found. Mildred Bliss wrote to offer her help. With resignation, Patterson replied, "I think [Farrand] is determined that there shall be no chance whatever that anyone will try to revitalize the original Reef Point project." Sadly, he was right.

Beatrix Farrand died in February 1959. Following her death, Bliss wished to pay tribute to her friend and organized the writing of a book about Farrand and her achievements. *Beatrix Jones Farrand, 1872–1959: An Appreciation of a Great Landscape Gardener* was privately published by Bliss in 1960. It includes articles by Robert Patterson, Mildred Bliss, and Lanning Roper, in addition to a list of Farrand's works. Bliss's article, "An Attempted Evocation of a Personality," begins, "In the death of Beatrix Farrand the American Society of Landscape Architects has lost the last surviving member of that farsighted and talented group which founded the Society ... and the world has lost a most unusual and a rarely gifted woman."

Above:
Ruth Havey's wrought-iron and gilt gates for the R Street facade, installed in 1954.

Above:
The R Street facade, c. 1922.

Left:
Beatrix Farrand's design for Arts and Crafts–style gates for the R Street facade.

Below:
Farrand's wooden gates, installed by 1930 and shown with finial mock-ups.

"Bang-Up Finale"

Back at Dumbarton Oaks, 1954 saw some slight changes to the garden. The yew hedges flanking the walk behind the tiled roofed tool sheds of the Kitchen Garden were replaced with forty *Prunus blireiana:* pink-flowering plum trees. They bloom in the early spring, even before the cherry blossoms. The luminous pale pink of the plum flowers echoes the hue of the hand-made Italian roof tiles. The path through the plums was renamed Prunus Walk.

In December 1954 replacement of the Arbor Terrace arbor was ordered. This magnificent structure, designed by Beatrix Farrand, had been adapted from the arbor at Château Montargis, designed by Jacques Androuet Du Cerceau, whose plans were published in Paris in the 1570s. Originally of oak, the reconstruction would be made out of Florida cypress by the Lank Woodwork Co., Inc., of Washington, D.C., and installed in 1955.

At the end of 1955, Robert Patterson retired from his work as consulting landscape architect after ten years at Dumbarton Oaks. He did, however, remain a member of the Garden Advisory Committee into the 1960s. On January 27, 1956, Jack Thacher wrote to landscape architect Alden Hopkins about the possibility of his becoming the new landscape consultant to Dumbarton Oaks, as well as its first garden fellow.

Hopkins, the resident landscape architect for Colonial Williamsburg, accepted Thacher's proposal. He was at that time a consultant to several similar public institutions, among them Monticello, Woodlawn Plantation, and the University of Virginia. In his initial evaluation of the garden, he quickly picked up on one of Mildred Bliss's new enthusiasms and specified that seventeen varieties of camellia, a total order of eighty-seven plants, be planted at Dumbarton Oaks that spring.

August 1956 found Mildred Bliss traveling in Italy. Ruth Havey wrote that the new arbor was in place and that she was prepared to order the wrought-iron Arbor Terrace balcony. As for the paved panel planned for the center of that terrace (its design modified and sundial-free), she adds, she has found "some beautiful great big chunks of Doria [stone] in Long Island City . . . I would like a plain center of the same gray crab orchard [stone] as the surrounding areas—for its sun and shade value—some gray-leaved woolly thyme which blooms white between the stones."

In Italy, Bliss made a point of visiting Bernard Berenson at his famous Villa I Tatti. There the landscape architect Cecil Pinsent had created a large black-and-white pebble mosaic terrace. Perhaps this design inspired Bliss to think about using the mosaic technique in her own garden. In Italy, she may also have seen the engraving of the master plan of the ground floor and garden of Palazzo Zenobio, a famous Venetian baroque garden, whose flat, flowing design closely suggests the future volutes of the Pebble Pool at Dumbarton Oaks.

It was not until the end of 1956 that Jack Thacher gave Hopkins a significant project: the Ellipse. The first phase in the redesign of the Ellipse, and the camellias, were to be Alden Hopkins's lasting contributions to Dumbarton Oaks.

Mildred Bliss, meanwhile, was still shopping for ornaments. On June 6, 1957, Dumbarton Oaks received one pair of "Sculptured Pineapple Ornaments—height 35 ½ inches" from a sale at Parke-Bernet. The pineapples were eventually installed at the bottom of the magnificent Box Walk where it enters the Ellipse.

Top:
View of the Pebble Pool under construction
from the Green Garden, c. 1961.

Above:
Mildred Bliss and Henry Du Pont
at the Pebble Pool.

"Several days ago we were shown through the gardens by Mrs. Robert Woods Bliss, who knows more about them than anyone else," reported Ami Stewart in a May 1958 article about touring the garden with Mildred Bliss. She continued:

We covered rather than skirted the boundary of the thirteen and a half acre gardens . . .

Down we went, pausing to admire a magnificent boxwood stairway—a deep green descent of about 60 or more feet—which was off to the left; or perhaps we stopped to inquire about the unusual hedge of large willow trees by the swimming pool. They had been clipped straight across the top and the long graceful branches were swinging in the summer breeze, making a lacy green veil over the blackness of the trunks. Mrs. Bliss told me that the designer of the gardens, Mrs. Beatrix Farrand, did many unusual things with trees and flowers, at times asking them to change their ways a bit in order to show a neighboring plant or just to change a little for the sake of grace.

As we walked through "melodious plot of beechen green and shadows numberless" Mrs. Bliss told me that many visitors had sought the beauty and solitude of such a small garden in Dumbarton Oaks to think over their problems and had found their answers. I remember Mrs. Bliss walking up to a shrub about eight feet high, touching it lightly and saying, "I am afraid you will have to go." She seemed to remember when each shrub or tree had been planted, and why each garden had been so planned.

In the midst of the gardens on our return, I stopped at a small pavilion on whose walls are prints of flowers and birds with their botanical and popular names. "This is my attempt at pedagogy," laughed Mrs. Bliss. Each month the flowers are changed to show the ones currently blooming and the children who visit the gardens can see the prints and the gardens in bloom.

In January 1959 Alden Hopkins sent Bliss two drawings: "one covering the reconstruction of the Camellia garden and one the proposed planting for the recently constructed Ellipse." He elaborated on his plans for the Ellipse in a letter to Jack Thacher: "My idea is to provide a fairly dense screen along the hill or south side . . . All are placed away from the aerial hornbeam hedge (*Carpinus caroliniana*) so that it will not be crowded. A . . . Japanese holly hedge with ultimate height of 4′ will give form and finish to the lower part of the Ellipse. A periwinkle border will hold spring bulbs. Other bulbs will be masses of color in the ivy ground cover." The hornbeams were trained into an aerial hedge, floating in the air like a thick letter O sixteen feet tall and fifteen feet across.

Mildred Bliss and Ruth Havey had started on another new scheme, Bliss's long-awaited "bang-up finale." In December 1959 Havey mailed an inquiry to Pioneer Pebble & Roofing Rock, Ltd., of Los Angeles: "I was interested to see your advertisement in the magazine 'Landscape'—showing Mexican beech pebbles in individual colors and sizes." Decorative use of pebble mosaic, a technique that dates back to the Romans, was used for the floor in the Star Garden and had been suggested by Beatrix Farrand in her *Plant Book:* "The ornamentation of the arches in the loggia will be interesting to work out, as designs in colored pebbles in stucco are not infrequent in Italian gardens."

Bliss and Havey began to play with the mosaic idea by creating small pebble pictures of cornucopias in the gravel panels on the Urn Terrace. These clumsy experiments were only a first step toward their ultimate goal—the complete redesign of the tennis court, which was positioned prominently just below the Green Garden. Havey wrote to Pioneer Pebbles: "There is an area 60′ x 120′

Above:
The antique fountain repositioned in the
center of the Ellipse.

Above:
Members of the Dumbarton Oaks staff installing objects in Philip Johnson's museum pavilion for Robert Bliss's collection of pre-Columbian art.

which will be made into a flowering parterre. In order to carry the pattern in the winter I would like to make the walks and the areas between the flower beds a pattern of pebbles in distinct colors—yellow, green, blue, red, black, white—any available color—but distinct colors—and pebbles flat enough to be set on edge and worked into distinct patterns."

By May 1960 Havey had revised the plan: "For the Tennis Court Parterre we have decided to build a larger pool than we had planned—as we have three very beautiful fountain figures in lead that should look well on a yellow and white floor in a shallow pool." Lawrence White originally contemplated buying the fountain figures, said to have come out of the Water Theater at Versailles, in 1927. But Irwin Laughlin, a Washington neighbor, bought another part of the set from the same dealer in Paris. In 1959 Mrs. S. W. Chandler, Laughlin's daughter, gave Dumbarton Oaks three of the rococo eighteenth-century figures: a Triton and two Amorini on hippocamps.

The Pebble Pool is a complex pattern of shallow pools, through which the pebbles glisten in rich ochers, whites, and grays. The three fountain figures are positioned to the north end of the design, while a pebble-patterned wheat sheaf is flanked by two carved-stone cornucopias that swirl to either side—the perfect symbol of the Blisses' bountiful life. This pool was completed in 1961.

Philip Johnson

By 1960 the gardens had a new professional adviser, Ralph E. Griswold, of Pittsburgh, Pennsylvania. His first task was to finish the redesign of the central fountain of the Ellipse.

Griswold's design—three lead masks (by a local sculptor, Don Turano) spouting water from their mouths into a pool—was developed with Mildred Bliss; the idea of the masks was mined from the Rateau design for the Bowling Green. The fountain was built but never considered a success and was soon replaced.

The present design for the Ellipse, also set within pleached hornbeams, places the antique Provençal fountain, which had originally been positioned in the Bosque, in the center of an elliptical pool. In 1962 the fountain was removed from the Bosque to clear the way for construction of the pre-Columbian museum.

Mildred Bliss, who had visited Foot's Cray gardens in Kent and requested the plan for the espaliered fruit-tree garden, asked Ralph Griswold to design a similarly elaborate espaliered fruit-tree garden for the Kitchen Garden area. But like the garden for the blind and the Byzantine garden, it was never built. Griswold retired from Dumbarton Oaks in 1962.

That same year Ruth Havey reported on another new project at Dumbarton Oaks: the preliminary research for the construction of a new garden library, to be designed by another old family friend, Frederick Rhinelander King, in the eighteenth-century French style. Havey assisted with the library's development. "The first step was to select the brick," she wrote Mildred Bliss. "We were lucky, I think, to find a good pink-red color that harmonizes with the color of the building." Havey designed the sidewalk ramp and "ribbon walk" that would lead to the library from the front of the house east toward the Garden Library. Obviously intended to be a main entrance, the ornate walk was never finished.

In 1961 the architect Philip Johnson, who is well known for his interest in landscape design, began work on a small museum pavilion for Dumbarton

Above:
Philip Johnson's museum pavilion.

Right:
Plan of the museum pavilion.

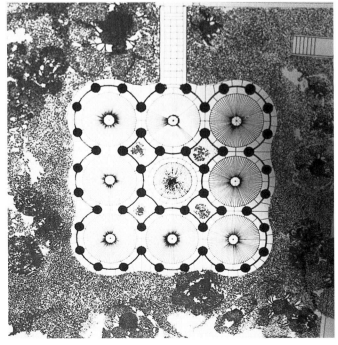

Oaks. Johnson had been selected by Jack Thacher, but he worked from the start in close collaboration with Mildred Bliss, whom he came to call his "co-architect." Made with glass walls that connect at stone columns, the pavilion seems to blend into the surrounding trees of the Bosque, the matte-finished putty-colored columns resembling thick tree trunks.

While the museum pavilion was under construction, Robert Bliss, now restricted to a wheelchair, would tour the site every afternoon. His collection of pre-Columbian art now fills the pavilion. Robert Bliss had fought one last battle for his country in the years prior to his death. In 1954, along with four other retired ambassadors, he had spoken out in a letter published in the *New York Times* against Senator Joseph McCarthy, who in the name of upholding "loyalty" and "moral standards" was encouraging members of the foreign service to in effect spy upon their colleagues. This practice, the ambassadors held, had a sinister effect that both undermined employees' confidence and smacked of totalitarianism.

Robert Bliss was now suffering from narcolepsy. He died at the age of eighty-seven. Astor Moore, the long-time cabinetmaker at Dumbarton Oaks, wrote of Robert and his involvement at the estate: "It's not to say that Mr. Bliss didn't have any taste, but he just left everything, all of the decisions, to her." Kenneth Clark wrote at the time of Robert Bliss's death:

At Dumbarton Oaks, and later at their house in Georgetown, they received their friends with a warmth, a style and an intelligence equal to that of the great salons of the eighteenth century ... Robert Bliss himself was a man of quiet charm and tolerance who listened modestly to the opinions of an endless stream of poets, diplomats, politicians and archaeologists from all over the world ... He was the best dressed man I have ever known: but one had the feeling that if he had been a poor man his life would have been equally civilized and harmonious.

Robert Woods Bliss left the bulk of his eleven-million-dollar estate to Harvard to be used as an endowment fund for the operations and maintenance of Dumbarton Oaks.

In his "Cityscape" column in the *Washington Post* in 1963, under the title "Dumbarton Pavilion's Scheme Is Inside Out," architectural critic Wolff Von Eckardt wrote:

There are occasions in our architecture for pomp and circumstance ... And there are occasions for intimate and quiet enjoyment of exquisite perfection, for the delight in a single flower.

Philip Johnson has given us such delight with his precious little pavilion in the beautiful garden park of Dumbarton Oaks ...

As the building went up, some Georgetowners grumbled that such an unusual structure—and a contemporary one, at that!—should be hidden from view. Now some of the same people complain that the wall and thick planting on 32nd St. all but cover a structure they have come to admire.

Wrote E. J. Applewhite in 1981:

In 1977 the Museum of Modern Art in New York held its first exhibition of contemporary architecture in over two decades ... The show presented over 400 buildings by more than 300 architects, and the city of Washington had no buildings represented in the entire show—except for Philip Johnson's Pre-Columbian Museum, an artifact of post-modernism's search for antecedents.

With considerably less attention, Frederick Rhinelander King's new Garden Library also opened its doors in 1963. The elegant library is furnished with antique furniture and nineteenth- and twentieth-century paintings, among them the Redon flowers from Beatrix Farrand, Edgar Degas' *The Song Rehearsal,* and Seurat's *Study of a Head.*

Quod Severis Metes

In the 1960s Royall Tyler's granddaughter Eve and her family moved to the Washington area. Eve Tyler Thompson was privileged to see a side of Mildred Bliss that few people knew. Once on Thompson's birthday, Bliss showed up at the door with a guitarist, who played and sang for the family all evening. Eve Thompson later discovered that the guitarist was renowned in France as the composer of songs of the French resistance. When Bliss finally became too frail to walk easily, she would have her driver take her to the Thompson house, where the whole family would pile into the limousine for a drive around the neighborhood. Occasionally when bored, Bliss would ask her driver to take her through Georgetown "to look at the hippies."

At Dumbarton Oaks, however, Bliss retained her aura as an empress, holding teas every afternoon with the scholars at Dumbarton Oaks—a "formal audience, part examination and part command performance," as Paul Richard described it in the *Washington Post.* "She would always wear white gloves and a hat," he wrote, "and watched [the scholars'] manners closely."

"I'm sure many people, especially scholars and academics, think this is top-heavy," said Mildred Bliss. "Only 25 scholars and all these gardens. It probably occurs to them that if there were no gardens, many more books could be bought!" But Bliss loved the gardens above all else. After visitors left the grounds for the day, she would walk out in the gardens, carrying with her a fringed parasol. Often she would sit alone on the balcony of the Arbor Terrace and would then generally work in the Garden Library until eight o'clock.

In January 1967 Mildred Bliss entered Doctor's Hospital in Washington, D.C., with a broken hip; later in the week she suffered a stroke from which she never recovered. Bliss died two years later, on January 17, 1969, at the age of eighty-nine. At her private funeral, held on R Street in Rock Creek Cemetery Chapel, white orchids covered her coffin as a string quartet played from behind a screen. Mildred Bliss's ashes then joined her husband Robert's in the wall of their favorite garden at Dumbarton Oaks, the Rose Garden. In 1969 Royall Tyler's son, William Tyler, replaced Jack Thacher as Dumbarton Oaks's director.

On April 16, 1969, the *Washington Post* announced:

Mildred C. Bliss, philanthropist and patron of the arts, left almost all of her $21 million estate to Harvard University for the advancement of its center at Dumbarton Oaks, the Georgetown estate where she lived for 20 years . . .

"These programs," the will says, should "Serve constructively to advance garden design and ornament through example, not just operate botany courses."

"I call upon the present and future presidents and fellows of Harvard college and all those who determine its policies," Mildred Bliss wrote in a preamble to her will, "to remember that Dumbarton Oaks is conceived in a new pattern . . . that it is the home of the humanities, not a mere aggregation of books and objects of art . . . Those responsible should remember . . . that gardens have their place in the Humanist order of life; and that trees are noble elements to be protected by successive generations and are not to be lightly destroyed."

Previous pages:
Lead wheat sheaf atop the Quod Severis
Metes bench in the Rose Garden; the Rose
Garden; view of the Pebble Pool from the
Green Garden.

Above:
View of the north facade of the house from
the North Vista.

Top:
The Orangery.

Above:
Stone ornaments surrounded by boxwood
by the south facade.

Following pages:
Nineteenth-century stone pineapples,
purchased by Robert and Mildred Bliss in
New York in 1957, at the junction between
the Box Walk and the Ellipse.

Above:
Carved stone urn on the Green Garden wall.

Opposite:
The Urn Terrace.

Following pages:
Path from the gatehouse inside the
R Street wall; the Terrior Column.

Epilogue

Like gardens everywhere, Dumbarton Oaks continues to grow and change. Perhaps the major difference from Mildred Bliss's time can be seen in the twenty-seven acres known as Dumbarton Oaks Park, the area to the north along the creek and in the woods, which was given to the United States Park Service in 1940.

A surrounding forest area, or "wilderness," was a common feature of eighteenth- and nineteenth-century American estates, but in most cases, this land was gradually sold, and as a result, very few examples remain. Dumbarton Oaks Park is a rare exception. It took a lot of work, and money, to maintain this idyllic "wilderness," even in Bliss's day. Erosion from the surrounding hills and the evidence of illegal dumping had to be removed annually; silting in the creek demanded at least a triannual clearing to keep the pools true to their "kalmia-leaf" configurations and the water flowing freely over the series of little waterfalls. Annuals, like the 150 primroses planted along the creek's banks, had to be replaced every spring. Throughout the park the rampant growth of vines and underbrush had to be vigorously cut back to allow more delicate plantings of laurel and rhododendron to thrive.

Once the land became the property of the Park Service, a shortage of manpower and funding precipitated a slow slide toward complete disorganization. That slide continued unchecked until 1992, when a group of people in the neighborhood and a handful of landscape architects formed the Friends of Montrose and Dumbarton Oaks Park, attracting the attention of both the Garden Conservancy and the National Park Service. In 1995 the group signed a cooperative agreement with the Park Service to work together to restore the park to its former character.

Friends "volunteer days" have already done much to clear away the underbrush; long-lost features, such as Beatrix Farrand's stone Mill Folly and the Grotto's pebble-paved waterway, although deteriorated, can be seen once again. The National Park Service has produced an impressive set of studies of the site, incorporating both historical data and surveys of existing plant material. In these studies are new scale drawings of some features in the park, including some hitherto unknown treasures that deserve to be restored to Beatrix Farrand's oeuvre.

After a bit of a lull, Dumbarton Oaks has recently begun to sharpen its image. Some of its sculptural features, lost to vandalism, have been brought back. A small bronze figure of Pan, the Greek god of shepherds and the forest, was cast and has been installed at the entrance to the Lovers Lane Pool.

Four paths lead from the woodland section of the estate into Dumbarton Oaks proper, but they were sealed off when the property was divided in 1940. In the fall of 1999, the portal to the main path, the Forsythia Arch, was repaired and reopened for a few hours, reuniting the two parts of the estate for the first time in close to sixty years.

The garden itself, under the careful attention of superintendent Gail Griffin, has evidenced a new fullness, and a little more flair: drawing on Mildred Bliss and Beatrix Farrand's experimental approach to planting schemes, Griffin has broadened the scope of what is now planted at Dumbarton Oaks using both research and her own intuition to fill in long-neglected spaces with plant material. In one instance, on the Fountain Terrace, she has added white Japanese anemones along the walls: the scheme does not show up in a planting plan, but the anemones do appear in an archival photograph from the 1930s.

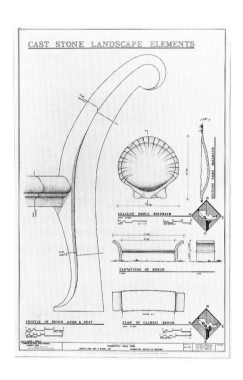

Above:
Scale drawing of a cast-stone bench and a shell-shaped birdbath from Dumbarton Oaks Park prepared by the National Park Service.

Opposite:
Superintendent Gail Griffin and the Dumbarton Oaks garden crew, 2000.

Following pages:
Cecil Beaton, photograph of Mildred Bliss, c. 1965.

Gail Griffin's approach follows most of the current interpretations of the garden, which no longer freeze its development with the departure of Beatrix Farrand in the early 1940s. This new way of interpreting the design views the garden as a more complex entity with Mildred Bliss's vision at its core, the single continuous thread in the first fifty years of the garden's development.

Mildred Bliss established the Garden Study Fellowships as a way for designers to learn about garden design and about her particular passion, ornament. But with landscape professionals focusing more on commercial designs, that focus never really took hold. In 1972 Dr. Elisabeth Blair MacDougall became the first director of the fellowship program, and under her direction, garden fellows at Dumbarton Oaks furthered their research into specific aspects of garden history. Annually in May, a garden history symposium brings garden scholars from around the world to Dumbarton Oaks. Over two days, papers are presented on such topics as Renaissance gardens, Islamic gardens, and even on the work of such twentieth-century designers as Beatrix Jones Farrand.

Although the scholarship of the fellows continues to be impressive and the symposiums enlightening, perhaps the most important contribution of the program has been something entirely unexpected: the development of a new science, garden archaeology. In 1979, at a Dumbarton Oaks symposium on ancient Roman gardens, Dr. Wilhelmina F. Jashemski presented a paper on her work in the gardens of ancient Pompeii. Because nothing living remains of these gardens, she adapted some archaeological techniques and invented others to gather her information. Jashemski's innovations included the analysis of pollen grains taken from soil samples and the plaster casting of tree-root cavities, both techniques she could use to identify plants that were grown nearly two thousand years ago.

Jashemski's presentation inspired a group of American landscape historians to apply her techniques to their projects. Among these was Dr. William Kelso, who was researching Thomas Jefferson's Monticello in Virginia. Kelso adapted Jashemski's techniques to American sites and, in the process, became an advocate for the new science. Today Jashemski's techniques are being used around the world; Mildred Bliss would undoubtedly be pleased with this circular development.

Following Mildred Bliss's death in 1969, there were a number of unexplained occurrences on the estate: open doors—doors that Bliss had always insisted on having closed—unaccountably slammed shut; a powerful, invisible presence at the "shack" caused workmen to run in fright from the premises. In the early 1970s a new member of the garden crew asked the superintendent about the elderly lady who carried a parasol and sat on the balcony of the Arbor Terrace each evening, just after the gardens closed to the public. Given all that Mildred Bliss accomplished in her life, and after, it wouldn't be a bit surprising.

Sources

Most of the documents cited are housed in Harvard University collections, either at the Pusey Library in Boston or at Dumbarton Oaks in Washington, D.C. Letters written by the Blisses and their family and friends are primarily from the Robert Bliss Collection and the Royall Tyler Collection at the Pusey Library. Letters between Mildred Bliss, Beatrix Farrand, and other garden advisors, as well as most archival drawings and photographs, are primarily from the collection at Dumbarton Oaks. Letters between Lawrence White, Robert Woods Bliss, Mildred Barnes Bliss, and Beatrix Jones Farrand are from the New-York Historical Society.

AAR: Franck Olivier-Vial and François Rateau. *Armand-Albert Rateau: Un Baroque Chez les Modernes.* Paris: Editions L'Amateur, 1992.

AARG: Patrick Chassé. *The Abby Aldrich Rockefeller Garden: A Visitor's Guide.* 1990.

AD: Victor Arwas. *Art Deco.* New York: Harry N. Abrams, 1980.

APW: Kenneth Clark. *Another Part of the Woods.* New York: Harper & Row, 1974.

AS: Douglass Shand-Tucci. *The Art of the Scandal: The Life and Times of Isabella Stewart Gardener.* New York: HarperCollins, 1997.

AW: Shane Leslie. *American Wonderland.* London: Michael Joseph, 1936.

BFAL: Diana Balmori, Diane Kostial McGuire, and Eleanor M. McPeck. *Beatrix Farrand's American Landscapes: Her Gardens & Campuses.* Sagaponack, N.Y.: Sagapress, 1985.

BFPB: Diane Kostial McGuire, ed. *Beatrix Farrand's Plant Book for Dumbarton Oaks.* Washington, D.C.: Dumbarton Oaks Trustees for Harvard University, 1980.

BG: Jane Brown. *Beatrix: The Gardening Life of Beatrix Jones Farrand, 1872–1959.* New York: Viking Penguin, 1995.

BJF: Beatrix Jones Farrand: Fifty Years of American Landscape Architecture. Washington, D.C.: Dumbarton Oaks, 1982.

BJHG: Mildred Bliss, Robert W. Patterson, and Lanning Roper. *Beatrix Jones and Her Gardens: An Appreciation of a Great Landscape Gardener.* Washington, D.C.: Mrs. Robert Woods Bliss, 1960.

C: Kenneth Clark. *Civilisation.* New York: Harper & Row, 1969.

DH: Edith Wharton and Ogden Codman Jr. *The Decoration of Houses.* 1897. New edition, New York: W. W. Norton, 1997.

DO: Beatrix Farrand. *Dumbarton Oaks.* Unpublished manuscript.

DOG: Beatrix Farrand. *Dumbarton Oaks Gardens.* Unpublished manuscript. Harvard University, Dumbarton Oaks, Washington, D.C., Garden Library and Rare Book Room.

DOGG: Georgina Masson. *Dumbarton Oaks: A Guide to the Gardens.* Washington, D.C.: Dumbarton Oaks/Trustees for Harvard University, 1968.

DOH: Walter Muir Whitehead. *Dumbarton Oaks: The History of the Georgetown House and Garden, 1800–1966.* Cambridge, Mass.: Belknap Press of Harvard University Press, 1967.

DOR: The Dumbarton Oaks Research Library and Collection, Harvard University, Bulletin Number One: 1940–1950. Washington, D.C.: Trustees for Harvard University/New York: Spiral Press, 1950.

EAI: Alan Price. *The End of the Age of Innocence: Edith Wharton and the First World War.* New York: St. Martin's Press, 1996.

EG: David Ottewill. *The Edwardian Garden.* New Haven and London: Yale University Press, 1989.

EW: R. W. B. Lewis. *Edith Wharton: A Biography.* New York: Fromm, 1985.

FW: Edith Wharton. *French Ways and Their Meaning.* 1919. New edition, Lee, Mass.: Edith Wharton Restoration at The Mount/Berkshire House Publishing, 1997.

GA: Eleanor Dwight. *The Gilded Age: Edith Wharton and Her Contemporaries,* New York: Universe, 1995.

GG: George Plumtre. *Great Gardens, Great Designers.* London: Ward Lock, 1996.

GO: Linda Lott. *Garden Ornament in the Dumbarton Oaks Garden: An Overview.* Washington, D.C.: Studies in Landscape Architecture, Dumbarton Oaks, Informal Papers, 1996.

GV: Alessandro Albrizzi and Mary Jane Pool. *The Gardens of Venice.* New York: Rizzoli, 1989.

HDO: Harvard University, Dumbarton Oaks, Washington, D.C., Garden Library and Rare Book Room.

HHG Harold Donaldson Eberlein and Cortland Van Dyke Hubbard. *Historic Houses of Georgetown and Washington, D.C.* Richmond, Va.: Dietz Press, 1958.

HPB: Harvard University, Pusey Library, Boston, Massachusetts, Harvard Archives: Bliss Archive.

HPT: Harvard University, Pusey Library, Boston, Massachusetts, Harvard Archives: Royall Tyler Papers.

IB: Edith Wharton. *Italian Backgrounds.* 1905. New edition, Hopewell, N.J: Ecco Press, 1989.

IV: Edith Wharton. *Italian Villas and Their Gardens.* 1904. New York: Da Capo/W. W. Norton, 1988.

JS: Elaine Kilmurray and Richard Ormond, eds. *John Singer Sargent.* London: Tate Gallery London, 1998.

LEW: R. W. B. Lewis and Nancy Lewis, eds. *The Letters of Edith Wharton.* New York: Collier Books/Macmillan, 1988.

MDO: John Thacher. *Music at Dumbarton Oaks: A Record 1940 to 1970.* 1977.

MLK: Martin Luther King Public Library, Washington, D.C.: Washingtonian Collection, *Washington Star* Archives.

NC: National Cyclopedia of American Biography, Being the History of the United States. New York: James T. White, 1958.

NPS: U.S. National Park Service, Department of the Interior, Washington, D.C., HABS No. DC-571: Dumbarton Oaks Park: Photographs, Reduced Copies of Measured Drawings, Written Historical Data, Historic American Buildings Survey, Library of Congress:

NYHS: New-York Historical Society, McKim, Mead, White Archives: Bliss file.

OSW: James M. Goode. *The Outdoor Sculpture of Washington, D.C.: A Comprehensive Historical Guide.* Washington, D.C.: Smithsonian Institution Press, 1974.

PM: Ignacy Jan Paderewski and Mary Lawton. *The Paderewski Memoirs.* New York: Charles Scribner's Sons, 1939.

PNA: Preservation Needs Assessment, Dumbarton Oaks Park, Washington, D.C. Washington, D.C.: George Washington University Historic Landscape Preservation Program, 1993.

RCHS: Records of the Columbia Historical Society, Martin Luther King Public Library, Washington, D.C.

RPB: Beatrix Farrand. *The Reef Point Bulletins.* 1946–56. New edition, Bar Harbor, Maine: Reef Point Gardens and Max Farrand Memorial Corporation, 1963.

RR: Anne Rockefeller Roberts. *Mr. Rockefeller's Roads: The Untold Story of Acadia's Carriage Roads & Their Creators.* Camden, Maine: Down East Books, 1990.

RS: Mrs. Winthrop "Daisy" Chandler. *Roman Spring.* 1934.

SO: Charles Annesley. *The Standard Operaglass.* New York: Tudor, 1934.

S: Robert Craft, ed. *Stravinsky: Selected Correspondence.* New York: Borzoi/Alfred A. Knopf, 1982.

TE: Robert Craft and Igor Stravinsky. *Themes & Episodes.* New York: Alfred A. Knopf, 1967.

TLA: Joachim Wolschke-Bulmahn, Angeliki E. Laiou, and Michel Conan. *Twenty-Five Years in Landscape Architecture at Dumbarton Oaks: From Italian Gardens to Theme Parks.* Washington, D.C.: Dumbarton Oaks Research Library and Collection, 1996.

UCB: University of California at Berkeley, College of Environmental Design, Beatrix Farrand/Reef Point Gardens Collections: manuscripts of lectures and articles.

W: E. J. Applewhite. *Washington, Itself: An Informal Guide to the Capital of the United States.* New York: Alfred A. Knopf, 1981.

Y: Yale University, Beinecke Rare Book and Manuscript Library, Yale Collection of American Literature, New Haven, Connecticut: Edith Wharton Collection.

Notes

Numbers preceding entries refer to page numbers.

ABB: Anna Dorinda Blakesley Barnes Bliss
BJF: Beatrix Jones Farrand
EW: Edith Wharton
JT: Jack Thacher
LW: Lawrence White
MBB: Mildred Barnes Bliss
RH: Ruth Havey
RP: Robert Patterson
RT: Royall Tyler
RWB: Robert Woods Bliss

Chapter One: 1920
24. "a watercolor fantasy": Olaf Graybar's sketchbook, HDO.
24. "Dumbarton Oaks is a garden": *BG*, p. 198.
25. "part of the unexpectedness": *AW*, p. 225.
25. "Perfect Bliss": *EW*, p. 372.
25. "a stern, wasp-waisted queen": Paul Richard, "Dumbarton Oaks: Reaching Out to Washington After 40 Years of Solitude," *Washington Post*, Aug. 26, 1979.
25. "It is the curse": MBB to BJF, July 13, 1922, HDO.
25. "There is no place": BJF to MBB, Nov. 13, 1940, HDO.
26. "She was a Virgo": Astor Moore, interview by author, Dumbarton Oaks, Washington, D.C., fall 1997.
27. "Her father, Demas Barnes": U.S. House of Representatives biographies, Legislative Resource Center, Washington, D.C., 1999.
27. "the artistic Anna": Unidentified obituary, HDO.
27. "Royall Tyler, the son of": HPT.
27. "the widowed and prosperous": "William Henry Bliss," *NC*, vol. 27, p. 29.
27. "You will prove your birthright": ABB to MBB, Oct. 17, 1897, HPB.
27. "An unenthusiastic student": HPB.
29. "A Catechism": HPB.
30. "with no reception": "Weds His Father's Wife's Daughter," *Daily Eagle*, Brooklyn, N.Y., Apr. 15, 1908, HPB.
30. "They then made an occasion": *DOH*, p. 59.
30. "Royall Tyler, now a brilliant": Annotated letters of RT to MBB, ed. Walter Muir Whitehead, HPT.
31. "[Royall's] sun is in conjunction": Prof. St. Leon's 1904 charts, HPB.
32. "Mildred's engagement book": MBB datebooks, HPB.
32. "stimulus for nearly forty years": MBB to Daisy Chandler, Sept. 14, 1937, HPT.
32. "Soon after reaching Paris": Ami Stewart, "New Wing at Dumbarton Oaks," unidentified newspaper clipping, HDO.
33. "Berenson, Gardner, and Edith Wharton": *AS*, p. 135.
33. "[Mildred] was also the brains": *EAI*, p. 26.
33. "American Distributing Service": HPB.
33. "I seem to poison": *EW*, p. 373.
34. "including, with Edith Wharton": EW to a friend, *LEW*, p. 346.
34. "The end of the world": MBB to "Lucy and Ernest," Paris, Aug. 24, 1916, HDO.
34. "Mr. and Mrs. Bliss": William Tyler annotations, HPT.
34. "the guest list came to include": Walter A. Tompkins, *News-Press* historian at HDO, undated article; brochure, collection of Nancy Wolff.
34. "the most agreeable and enjoyable": *PM*, p. 209.
35. "Both Blisses received innumerable honors": Awards list, HPB.
35. "It had always been my dream": RWB, lecture to Harvard Club, Washington, D.C., Apr. 8, 1943, HPB.
35. "I can sense the emotions": RWB to MBB, June 6, June 8, 1920, HDO.
36. "The Oaks had originally": Hugh H. Taggart, "Old Georgetown"; Cordelia Jackson, "People and Places in Old Georgetown"; Mary A. Mitchell, "An Intimate Journey Through Georgetown"; Mathilde D. Williams, "Old Georgetown as Chronicled in Peabody Collection"; William A. Gordon, "Old Homes on Georgetown Heights"; all in *RCHS; HHG*, p. 165; Charles M. Wiltse, "The Calhouns at Dumbarton Oaks," MLK.
37. "Robert mentioned two specific features": *Washington Star*, Mar. 25, 1956.
37. "superb location and the fine trees": *DOH*, p. 62.
37. "before alterations were made": *DOG*.
39. "After we had bought the place": *Times-Herald*, Nov. 3, 1940, MLK.
40. "those bricks probably came": *Washington Star*, Mar. 25, 1956.
40. "The Philadelphia metalsmith": Samuel Yellin archives, Philadelphia, Pa.
40. "Mildred Bliss invited Beatrix Jones Farrand": Date of BJF's first visit to DO from MBB datebooks, HPB.

Chapter Two: 1921–1922
42. "Tuesday, January 25, 1921": MBB datebooks, HPB.
42. "Farrand at the time was busy": *BG*, pp. 26, 203–16.
42. "the majority of the artists and architects": James Carder, interview by author, Dumbarton Oaks, Washington, D.C., Dec. 1998.
42. "Mrs. Bliss knew from the start": Lanning Roper, "Dumbarton Oaks: A Great American Garden," *BJHG;* "Perfection in Detail," *Country Life*, Jan. 3–10, 1974.
43. "the character in Maurice Maeterlinck's play": *SO*, p. 566.
46. "It is important that their curbs": *BFPB*, p. 69.
47. "The onrush of spring": MBB, "An Attempted Evocation of a Personality," *BJHG*.
47. "The late Lord Aberconway": Lanning Roper, "Dumbarton Oaks: A Great American Garden," *BJHG*.
49. "Your letter and its enclosure": MBB to BJF, July 13, 1922, HDO.
49. "I don't like the idea": EW to Max Farrand, Oct. 3, 1922, Y.

50. "Farrand's professional fees": Diana Balmori, interview by author, New Haven, Conn., summer 1999.

50. "Her authority was so complete": Robert Patterson, "Beatrix Cadwallader Jones," *BJHG*.

50. "Landscape architecture or gardening": BJF, two unpublished lectures, UCB.

Chapter Three: 1922–1932

84. "Lawrence G. White of the Manhattan architectural firm": MBB datebooks, HPB.

84. "a wave of trained estate gardeners": *EG*.

84. "Since his return to the United States": *Washington Herald,* undated clipping (c. Jan. 1923), HPB.

86. "contain a collection of orchids": Donald Smith, interview by author, Bar Harbor, Maine, Sept. 1997.

86. "The trees had to be 'honored'" : Philip Johnson, interview by author, New Canaan, Conn., Mar. 1997 and Jan. 1999.

86. "The inherent beauty of the garden": *IV*, p. 8.

86. "When the Blisses bought The Oaks": Michel Conan, interview by author, Dumbarton Oaks, Washington, D.C., June 1999.

87. "The arts of architecture": BJF, "The Garden in Relation to the House," *Garden in Forest*, Apr. 7, 1897, UCB.

88. "How delightfully & intelligently": EW to BJF, July 23, 1923, Y.

88. "On either side of the walk": *BJPF*, p. 26.

89. "Prices were determined": LW estimates, NYHS.

89. "My dear White, I am sorry": RWB to LW, Apr. 19, 1924, NYHS.

89. "Have you any idea": LW to BJF, May 5, 1924, NYHS.

89. "the letter covers eight different points": BJF to LW, Dec. 9. 1924, NYHS.

90. "The path, called Mélisande's Allée": Giorgio Galletti, interview by author, Dumbarton Oaks, Washington, D.C., Nov. 1998.

90. "It is . . . necessary to keep this walk": *BFPB*, p. 103.

93. "I suppose 'aloof' is a fair description": Robert Patterson to Jennifer Goodman, Jan. 22, 1986, collection of Robert Patterson.

93. "she may have suffered": *BG*, p. 88.

93. "Farrand once explained that her love of gardening": *RPB*, vol. 1, no. 17.

93. "Professor Charles Sprague Sargent, first director": *JS*, p. 11.

94. "the grateful guest of Mrs. Sargent": *RPB*, vol. 1, no. 17.

94. "Make the plan fit the ground": BJF, two unpublished lectures, UCB.

94. "She kept a diary of her impressions": BJF notebooks, UCB.

96. "Details of materials and patterns": Lanning Roper, "Dumbarton Oaks: A Great American Garden," *BJHG*.

96. "Farrand's second challenge at The Oaks": Michel Conan, interview by author, Dumbarton Oaks, Washington, D.C., June 1999.

98. "the Blisses had initiated a push": *EW*, p. 482.

99. "These seats have been adapted": *BFPB*, pp. 107–8.

99. "a precedent for the two squat garden pavilions": *BG*, p. 140.

99. "The whole place looks ravishingly lovely": LW to RWB, May 4, 1927, NYHS.

101. "Rateau was one of the least known": *AAR*, p. 149.

102. "Rateau, in turn, produced some thirty-two": HDO.

102. "I knew that [at Dumbarton Oaks] Rateau had been": James Carder, interview by author, Dumbarton Oaks, Washington, D.C., Dec. 1998.

102. "Farrand had suddenly lost a good deal": *BG*, p. 149.

107. "Never in all the years did [Farrand]": MBB, "An Attempted Evocation of a Personality," *BJHG*.

Chapter Four: 1933–1937

140. "arborists were brought in every few years": Donald Smith, interview by author, Bar Harbor, Maine, Sept. 1997.

140. "The first party logged": MBB, dinner party record, HPB.

142. "Your letter from Georgetown": EW to BJF, Aug. 3, 1933, Y.

142. "When we were living in Argentina": MBB to Mr. Hauck, May 8, 1941, HDO.

142. "Since our return . . . we have hardly had": MBB to Mrs. John L. (Polly) Bonney, Sept. 8, 1934, HPB.

143. "It is a revelation of course": Dorothy Elmhurst writing to MBB on Sept. 13, 1933, signed "Dorothy" at HPB.

143. "The Box Ellipse is one of the quietest": *BFPB*, p. 78.

143. "The photographs from Dumbarton Oaks": EW to BJF, Oct. 29, 1935, Y.

146. "a place designed for more-or-less intimate": *BFPB*, p. 34.

146. "I stopped to see Mildred at Santa Barbara": BJF to EW, undated letter, Y.

146. "Mildred looked very thin": EW to BJF, Apr. 17, 1936, Y.

146. "Our little Madeiran gardener": BJF to EW, Oct. 24, 1936, Y.

147. "But when I met her again": *APW,* p. 203–4.

147. "And suddenly all that Anglo-American mahogany": James Carder, interview by author, Dumbarton Oaks, Washington, D.C., Dec. 1998.

149. "that machine of perfect precision": MBB to Daisy Chandler, HPB.

149. "Across [the Pont des Arts in Paris] for the last one hundred and fifty years": *C*, p. 1.

149. "You have been more than usually in our thoughts": MBB to Daisy Chandler, Sept. 14, 1937, HPB.

Chapter Five: 1938–1947

150. "For ten days I've been hearing": Jean Eliot, "Rumors Give Bliss House to Harvard," *Washington Herald*, Jan. 16, 1938, MLK.

152. "The Rose Garden was first thought of": Michel Conan, interview by author, Dumbarton Oaks, Washington, D.C., June 1999.

152. "As for the colors of the rose garden": BJF to MBB, July 7, 1922, HDO.

152. "Nothing makes a better background": *BFPB*, p. 63.

152. "One with the pediment broken": RH to MBB, Dec. 7, 1937, HDO.

152. "He died as he had lived": MBB to BJF, Jan. 3, 1938, HDO.

153. "Dumbarton Oaks has entered upon a new development": MBB to BJF, Mar. 16, 1938, HDO.

153. "[It] is a copy of one seen in a garden": BJF to Anne Sweeney, June 19, 1944, HDO.

154. "By all means let us follow your inspired idea": BJF to MBB, May 26, 1938, HDO.

154. "The Dumbarton Oaks gardens were open": "Garden Open October 22," *Washington Times*, Oct. 6, 1938, MLK.

154. "These concerts were later continued": *MDO*, p. vii.

155. "The primroses were especially pretty": Bryce to BJF, referred to in BJF to MBB, May 2, 1939, HDO.

155. "Annually 150 candelabra primroses": NPS, p. 43.

155. "Please . . . be an angel": MBB to Caroline Phillips, Sept. 27, 1939, HPB.

155. "The inscription on the bench": *GO*, p. 34.

155. "I hardly feel capable": Caroline Phillips to MBB, Oct. 4, 1939, HPB.

157. "Your gallant self-discipline": MBB to BJF, Jan. 27, 1940, HDO.

157. "Foreigners were particularly interested": Katherine Brooks, "Scientific Congress Delegates Are Received at Dumbarton Oaks: Former Ambassador and Mrs. Bliss Are Delightful Hosts Amid Beauties of Vast Garden," *Washington Star*, May 17, 1940, MLK.

157. "The weeks pass—agonizing weeks": MBB to BJF, July 24, 1940, HDO.

158. "Whether you pronounce BIZ-an-tin": Hope Ridings Miller, "Capitalites," *Washington Post*, Nov. 2, 1940, MLK.

158. "Bernard Berenson sent a telegram": HPB.

158. "Max Farrand made the announcement": "Dr. Farrand Resignation Accepted," *Star-News*, undated clipping, HPB.

158. "How strange our parallel decision": MBB to BJF, Nov. 20, 1940, HDO.

158. "Bliss Estate Transferred to Harvard": Gerald G. Gross, "Blisses Sign Deeds Transferring Estate," *Washington Times-Herald*, Dec. 1, 1940, MLK.

159. "We felt that inevitably the United States": "Dumbarton Oaks Capital Landmark," *Washington Star*, Mar. 25, 1956.

159. "They seemed to feel that visit": BJF to MBB, telegram, Jan. 18, 1941, HDO.

159. "She began to prepare a garden book": BJF to Anne Sweeney, Feb. 16, 1941, HDO.

159. "You and I both know what a busy pair": BJF to Anne Sweeney, July 12, 1941, HDO.

160. "Dear Mrs. Heifetz": MBB to Mrs. Heifetz, Sept. 4, 1941, HPB.

160. "A remarkable thing happened here": John White, "What Goes On at Dumbarton Oaks: The Story of Year One of a Strange Project," *Washington Times-Herald*, Nov. 30, 1941, MLK.

160. "We are, at last, definitely going eastward": MBB to BJF, May 14, 1942, HDO.

162. "The Bride magnolia was in excellent condition": "Mrs. Bliss and Park Dept. and Bryce D.O. Agenda," "Mrs. Bliss, Mr. Thacher and Bryce," meeting agendas, June 2, 1942, HDO.

162. "Suggest to Mrs. Bliss a possibility": JT, "Memorandum for Executive Committee, Re Mrs. Farrand," Sept. 25, 1942, HDO.

162. "My very dearest . . . To keep the balance": BJF to MBB, June 17, 1942, HDO.

162. "Haveylet and I earnestly working": BJF to MBB, telegram, June 25, 194, HDO..

162. "Bryce tells me you find the garden": BJF to MBB, Feb. 16, 1943, HDO.

163. "The shack": Donald Smith, interview by author, Bar Harbor, Maine, Sept. 1998.

163. "The end of May last year": RWB, address to the Harvard Club, text dated Apr. 8, 1943, HPB.

163. "There was a time when an invitation": Evelyn Peyton Gordon, "Uncle Sam's WAVES Model Best Designs of Mr. Mainbocher," *Washington Daily News*, July 24, 1944, MLK.

163. "'Peace' is the watchword": Joseph H. Baird, "Dumbarton Oaks Estate Offers Peaceful Setting for 'Big Four' Talks: Security Conference of Major Powers Conductive to Both Work and Relaxation," *Washington Star*, Aug. 1, 1944, MLK.

163. "This, it seems to me, is of such importance": MBB to BJF, Aug. 19, 1944, HDO.

163. "The last years have taken their toll": BJF to MBB, Apr. 1, 1946, HDO.

164. "need the time to absorb": BJF to MBB, May 15, 1946, HDO.

164. "I have had several talks with Mrs. Farrand": RP to JT, June 11, 1946, HDO.

164. "I went over your June 11th letter": MBB to BJF, July 26, 1946, HDO.

164. "You may have forgotten": BJF to MBB, Oct. 14, 1946, HDO.

165. "You will, I feel sure . . . make Dumbarton": "Dumbarton Oaks: February 3rd through February 6th, 1947 (R.W.P., Mr. Thacher, Mrs. Bliss, Miss Sweeney, Mr. Bryce)," HDO.

165. "The two together propound": BJF to MBB, Feb. 28, 1947, HDO.
165. "I read it and thought it": MBB to BJF, Mar. 22, 1947, HDO.
166. "Would like me to continue": BJF to MBB, Apr. 7, 1947, HDO.

Chapter Six: 1947–1969

184. "A total of 17,198 visitors": "Report on Dumbarton Oaks Garden Tours, Spring Season: 1947, April 15th to and including June 29th," HDO.
184. "as no other place has": BJF to MBB, May 26, 1947, HDO.
184. "subject of the moment is the Garden Center": RP to JT, Aug. 5, 1947, HDO.
184. "a fire swept": Donald Smith, interview by author, Bar Harbor, Maine, Sept. 1998.
184. "the entire output of Gertrude Jekyll's long": BJF to MBB, May 24, 1948, HDO.
184. "I should like nothing better": MBB to BJF, July 26, 1948, HDO.
185. "I am still trying to get at [Farrand's] files": RP to JT, Apr. 29, 1948, collection of Robert Patterson.
185. "Mrs. Farrand has, of her own accord": RP to JT, Oct. 19, 1948, collection of Robert Patterson.
185. "The model for the Melisande Steps": RH to MBB, July 17, 1949, HDO.
185. "Some of the 'bones' of the design": Ami Stewart, "The Dumbarton Oaks Gardens Present May's Roses," unidentified newspaper clipping, May 22, 1958, MLK.
185. "Just as soon as the right specification": MBB to RH, Aug. 12, 1949, HDO.
186. "A peaceful Sunday morning": Henry Du Pont to MBB, Nov. 16, 1949, HPB.
186. "to break the provisions ": BJF writing to MBB about Harvard and the Arnold Arboretum in a letter dated Mar. 18, 1950 at HDO.
186. "Much of my heart": BJF to MBB, May 1, 1950, HDO.
186. "I am constantly alert": MBB to BJF, May 1950, HDO.
186. "an extreme improvement": JT to RP, Dec. 28, 1949, HDO.
186. "All things considered": MBB to RH, Sept. 13, 1950, HDO.
186. "[Doctors'] orders are orders": BJF to MBB, Jan. 11, 1951, HPB.
186. "to my eyes looks well": JT to RP, Apr. 4, 1951, HDO.
189. "Mildred Bliss had begun a push": JT to RP, Aug. 6, 1951, collection of Robert Patterson; MBB to BJF, Mar. 16, 1952, HDO.
189. "What, he asked Jack Thacher, would a fellow": JT to RP, Aug. 6, 1951, collection of Robert Patterson.
189. "Robert Patterson recommended that": RP to JT, Feb. 5, 1952, HDO.
189. "singularly complicated": MBB to BJF, Mar. 16, 1952, HDO.
189. "What a good time we had": BJF to MBB, Jan. 9, 1953, HDO.
189. "A bill from R. B. Phelps Cut Stone": Bill, May 21, 1953, HDO.
190. "I hardly know where to start": RH to MBB, Jan. 7, 1954, HPB.
190. "I really think it did": RP to JT, Sept. 24, 1954, collection of Robert Patterson.
190. "There was no financial necessity": RP to JT, Sept. 26, 1955, HPB.
190. "In the death of Beatrix Farrand": *BJHG,* p. 9.
192. "arbor at Château Montargis": *GO,* p. 17.
192. "he quickly picked up on": Alden Hopkins, report on Dumbarton Oaks, Mar. 22 and 23, 1956, HDO.
192. "some beautiful great big chunks": RH to MBB, Aug. 12, 1956, HDO.
192. "Bliss made a point of visiting": Bernard Berenson to MBB, postcard, Aug. 7, 1956, HPB.
192. "master plan of the ground floor": *GV,* p. 139.
192. "Sculptured Pineapple Ornaments": Invoice from Bruce Butterfield, Inc., June 6, 1957, HDO.
194. "Several days ago we were shown": Ami Stewart, "The Dumbarton Oaks Gardens Present May's Roses," unidentified newspaper clipping, May 22, 1958, MLK.
194. "My idea is to provide": Alden Hopkins, report to Garden Advisory Committee, Jan. 20, 1959, HDO.
194. "I was interested to see": RH to Pioneer Pebbles & Roofing Rock, Inc., Dec. 4, 1959, RH file at HDO.
194. "The ornamentation of the arches": *BFPB,* p. 47.
197. "Griswold's design—three lead masks": Unidentified article, *Washington Star,* June 2, 1963, MLK.
197. "Mildred Bliss, who had visited Foot's Cray": Plan of Foot's Cray, HDO.
198. "Johnson had been selected": Philip Johnson, interview by author, New Canaan, Conn., Mar. 1997 and Jan. 1999.
198. "Robert Bliss had fought": RWB with Norman Arnour, Joseph C. Grew, William Phillips, and G. Howland Shaw, "Backing Our Diplomats," *New York Times,* Jan. 17, 1954, HPB.
198. "It's not to say that": Astor Moore, interview by author, Dumbarton Oaks, Washington, D.C., fall 1997.
198. "At Dumbarton Oaks, and later": Kenneth Clark, obituary of RWB, unidentified newspaper clipping, HPB.
198. "Robert Woods Bliss left": RWB, will, HPB.
198. "There are occasions": Wolff Von Eckardt, "Dumbarton Pavilion's Scheme is Inside Out," *Washington Post,* undated article (ca. 1963), MLK.

198. "In 1977 the Museum of Modern Art": *W,* p. 293.
200. "Once on Thompson's birthday": Eve Tyler Thompson, interview by author, Bethesda, Md., Feb. 1999.
200. "formal audience, part examination": Paul Richard, "Dumbarton Oaks: Reaching Out to Washington After 40 Years of Solitude," *Washington Post,* Aug. 26, 1979.
200. "I'm sure many people": Selwa Roosevelt, "Dumbarton Oaks Capital Landmark," *Washington Star,* Mar. 25, 1956.
200. "At her private funeral": Astor Moore, interview by author, Dumbarton Oaks, Washington, D.C., fall 1997.
200. "Mildred C. Bliss, philanthropist": Thomas J. Lippman, "Dumbarton Oaks to Receive $20 Million from Bliss Will," *Washington Post,* Apr. 16, 1969.
200. "I call upon the present": MBB, will (copy), collection of Robert Patterson.

Epilogue
218. "The National Park Service has produced": U.S. National Park Service studies, NPS.
219. "drawing on Mildred Bliss": Gail Griffin, interview by author, Dumbarton Oaks, Washington, D.C., Feb. 1999.
219. "the development of a new science": Susan Tamulevich, "Plotting the Garden," *Inform,* Mar./Apr. 1991.
219. "Jashemski's presentation inspired": William Kelso, interview by author, Mount Vernon, Va., Jan. 1991.

Illustration Credits

All photographs, except as noted below, are by Ping Amranand. Numbers refer to page numbers.

Beinecke Library, Yale University: 143 top

Bliss Papers, Pusey Archives of Harvard University: 27 top, 28 bottom left, 28 top right, 28 bottom right, 30, 34, 35, 88, 141 bottom, 146 top, 167, 193 bottom, 220–21

Dumbarton Oaks, Trustees for Harvard University: 23, 24, 27 bottom, 28 top left, 36, 38 top, 38, 41 top, 43, 44, 46, 85, 87, 91 top, 92, 96, 97, 98, 99, 100, 101, 102, 103, 104, 105, 106, 140, 141 top, 143 bottom, 144, 145, 148, 149, 151, 152, 153, 154, 156, 161, 165, 187, 188, 190, 191, 193 top, 194, 195, 196, 219 (photograph by Joe Mills)

Beatrix Jones Farrand Collection (1955-2) Environmental Design Archives, University of California, Berkeley: 48, 146 bottom

Historical American Buildings Survey, National Park Service, Library of Congress: 218

Courtesy Evelyn Hofer: 201

Courtesy Philip Johnson: 198

New-York Historical Society: 91 center and bottom

Smith College Archives: 185

Yale University Art Gallery, Yale University, gift of Mrs. Dixon Stroud: 93

Courtesy Claire Yellin, Samuel Yellin Metalworks Co. archive, Bryn Mawr, Pennsylvania: 40, 41 bottom

Dumbarton Oaks Plan

Large dates refer to the date of original construction or major modification. Small dates refer to modification or renovation.

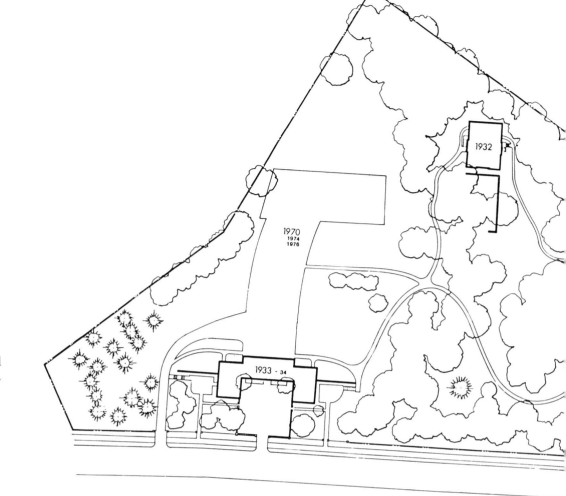

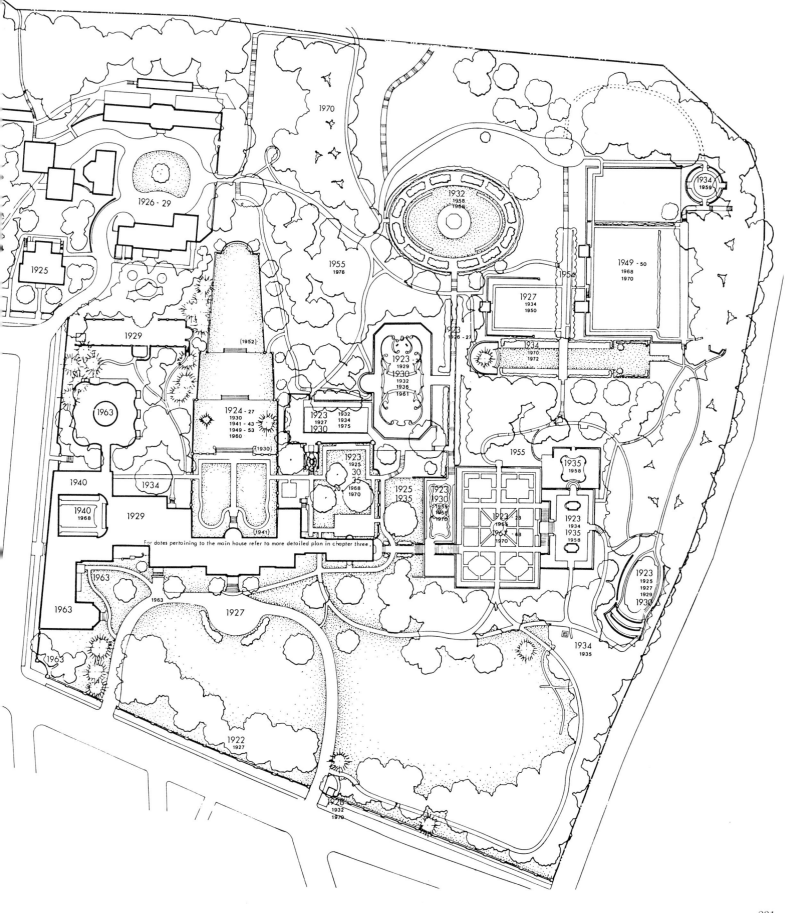